HEALING TRAUMA

Finding Peace After
Pain

Amara Lynn

Table of Contents

Introduction

First of all, I want to say something really important: I see you. I see the pain you're carrying, the weight on your shoulders, and the courage it took for you to open this book. You're here because something in your life shifted, and left a mark—a mark that may feel too deep to heal or too overwhelming to confront. I understand, and I want you to know that you're not alone.

My name is Amara, and I want to share something very personal with you. When I was just 17 years old, I experienced a profound loss that changed my life in ways I could never have anticipated. My mum, who was not just my parent but my guiding star, passed away. She was a single parent, the center of our small family, and losing her was like having the ground ripped out from under me. Suddenly, I was thrust into the role of caretaker for my two younger siblings, facing responsibilities that seemed too vast for my teenage self. I was overwhelmed, grieving, and trying to navigate the chaos of my new reality.

The journey was anything but easy. I found myself grappling with what's often called "eldest daughter syndrome," a term that describes the unspoken expectations placed on the eldest child to be the strong one, the responsible one, the one who holds everything together. For me, this meant juggling my own grief with the constant demands of caregiving, all while trying to figure out who I was in the midst of all this upheaval.

I know that many of you might be feeling something similar—a heavy burden, a sense of being overwhelmed, or perhaps a feeling of being lost in the midst of your pain. I want you to know that it's okay to feel this way. It's okay to acknowledge that you're struggling, and it's okay to seek help and healing. This book is here to walk with you on that journey.

I've written this book not just as a guide but as a companion. I want to share with you the lessons I've learned, the struggles I've faced, and the ways I've found to heal and move forward. My hope is that by sharing my story and the insights I've gained along the way, I can offer you some comfort and encouragement. I want this to be a place where you can find understanding and hope, where you can see that even in the darkest moments, there is a path to healing.

You might be wondering what healing really means and how it's possible to find peace after such deep pain. Healing isn't about forgetting or erasing the past. It's about finding a way to live fully and authentically despite the scars we carry. It's about acknowledging our pain, understanding it, and learning how to integrate it into our lives in a way that allows us to move forward with hope and purpose.

I want to emphasize that this book is not a quick-fix solution. Healing is a journey, and it's one that takes time, patience, and self-compassion. There will be moments when it feels like you're taking one step forward and two steps back, and that's okay. What matters is that you keep moving, even if it's at a pace that feels slow. Every step, no matter how small, is progress.

As you read through these pages, I encourage you to take your time. Reflect on your own experiences, relate to the stories I share, and use the knowledge to explore your own path to healing. Remember that your feelings are valid, your pain is real, and your journey is uniquely yours. Healing is not about achieving perfection; it's about finding a sense of peace and acceptance within yourself.

I hope that this book serves as a beacon of hope, a reminder that healing is possible, and a guide to finding peace after pain. You don't have to walk this path alone—there are others who understand, and there are ways to find light even in the darkest times.

Thank you for allowing me to be a part of your journey. Let's take this first step together, with hope in our hearts and the belief that brighter days are ahead.

What to Expect

I want to give you a clear picture of what you can expect from this book. My goal is to guide you through your own path to healing with compassion, understanding, and practical advice. Healing from trauma is a deeply personal process, and while every journey is unique, there are certain themes and tools that can help you along the way. Here's a look at what this book will cover and how it's designed to support you in finding peace after trauma.

Understanding Trauma: What It Is and How It Affects Us

We'll start by diving into what trauma really is. You might have heard the term "trauma" used in various contexts, but what does it actually mean in the context of emotional and psychological healing? Trauma isn't just about dramatic or catastrophic events; it's about how these events impact us on a deep, emotional level. We'll explore the different types of trauma, from acute to complex, and discuss how they can affect our mental and physical health.

Understanding trauma is the first step in healing. It helps to know why you might be feeling certain things and how trauma can influence your reactions, behaviors, and relationships. We'll look at the science behind trauma, including how it affects the brain and body, and why healing takes time. This foundational knowledge can provide comfort and clarity, helping you understand that your responses are natural and that healing is possible.

Acknowledging Your Pain: The Importance of Facing Your Feelings

One of the most challenging aspects of healing is facing the pain. It's often easier to push our emotions aside or to put on a brave face, but true healing begins with acknowledging and accepting your feelings. We'll talk about why it's important to allow yourself to grieve, to feel anger, sadness, or even numbness, and how to do this in a healthy, constructive way.

You'll learn strategies for recognizing and processing your emotions, including journaling, mindfulness, and therapy. These tools can help you to give voice to your pain, understand it better, and start working through it. Remember, it's okay to feel what you're feeling, and it's a crucial part of the healing process.

Practical Steps for Healing: Building Your Toolbox

Healing isn't just about understanding trauma or acknowledging your pain; it's also about taking actionable steps to support your recovery. In this section, we'll explore practical strategies that can help you on your journey to healing. This includes self-care practices, coping mechanisms, and lifestyle changes that can support your emotional well-being.

We'll discuss the importance of self-care and how to build a routine that nurtures your physical and emotional health. You'll find tips on creating a supportive environment, setting boundaries, and finding healthy ways to cope with stress and anxiety. I'll also share exercises and activities that have helped me and others on their healing journeys.

Finding Support: The Role of Community and Professional Help

No one has to go through healing alone. Finding support is a crucial part of the recovery process, and we'll explore different ways to build a supportive network. Whether it's reaching out to friends and family, joining support groups, or seeking professional help, having a support system can make a significant difference.

We'll discuss how to find the right therapist or counselor, the benefits of group therapy, and how to lean on your community. You'll also learn about the importance of connecting with others who understand your experiences, and how sharing your journey can be both healing and empowering.

Embracing Forgiveness: Letting Go of the Past

Forgiveness is a powerful tool in the healing process. It's often misunderstood as condoning or forgetting what happened, but in reality, forgiveness is about freeing yourself from the hold that past pain has on you. We'll explore what forgiveness really means and how it can help you move forward.

You'll learn about the benefits of forgiving others, as well as yourself. We'll discuss techniques for letting go of resentment and anger, and how to work towards a place of inner peace. Forgiveness can be a challenging process, but it's a crucial step in finding freedom from the past.

Building Resilience: Strengthening Your Inner Strength

Resilience is the ability to bounce back from adversity, and it's a skill that can be developed and strengthened over time. We'll talk about what resilience is, how it can be cultivated, and why it's so important in the healing process. You'll find strategies for building your resilience, including developing a growth mindset, practicing gratitude, and finding meaning in your experiences.

You'll also learn about the role of self-compassion and how it contributes to resilience. By treating yourself with kindness and understanding, you'll be better equipped to face challenges and build a more resilient mindset.

Moving Forward: Creating a Vision for Your Future

Healing is not just about dealing with the past; it's also about looking towards the future with hope and purpose. In this section, we'll focus on how to create a vision for your life after trauma. This includes setting goals, finding new sources of joy, and redefining your sense of purpose.

We'll explore ways to envision a future that aligns with your values and aspirations. You'll learn how to set realistic and meaningful goals, and how to take steps towards achieving them. This is about building a life that feels fulfilling and aligned with who you are becoming.

Celebrating Your Journey: Acknowledging Progress and Growth

Throughout the healing process, it's important to recognize and celebrate your progress. Healing is not a destination but a journey, and every step you take is a victory. We'll discuss how to acknowledge and celebrate your achievements, no matter how small they may seem.

You'll find encouragement to reflect on your journey, appreciate how far you've come, and recognize the strength and resilience you've developed. Celebrating your progress can provide motivation and reinforce your commitment to continuing on your path to healing.

As you move through this book, you can expect to find a blend of personal stories, practical advice, and inspirational guidance. My goal is to provide you with the tools and support you need to navigate your own healing journey with hope and confidence. Healing from trauma is a deeply personal process, and while the path may not always be smooth, there is light at the end of the tunnel.

This book is here to walk with you every step of the way, offering insights, encouragement, and practical strategies to help you find peace and reclaim your life. Healing is possible, and with each chapter, I hope to inspire you to take steps towards a brighter, more fulfilling future.

Understanding Trauma

Let's start at the very beginning—what is trauma? It's a term that gets thrown around a lot, but understanding it deeply can help us make sense of what we've been through and how we can start to heal. Grab a cup of tea, get comfortable, and let's unpack this together.

The Basics of Trauma

Trauma is a word we often hear in discussions about mental health, but its meaning can vary widely. At its core, trauma refers to an emotional response to an event or series of events that deeply impacts our sense of safety, well-being, and identity. It's not just about the event itself but also about how we process and react to it.

To better understand trauma, it's important to recognize that it can take many forms. The nature of the event or experience isn't as significant as how it affects the individual. Two people might go through the same event but react to it very differently. This is because trauma is deeply personal and influenced by a variety of factors, including our past experiences, support systems, and inherent resilience.

Here are the different types of trauma:

Acute Trauma: This type of trauma results from a single, distressing event that happens suddenly and is often shocking. Examples include car accidents, natural disasters, or witnessing a violent incident. These events can leave us feeling shocked, overwhelmed, and unable to process what has happened. The emotional impact of acute trauma can be immediate and intense, leading to symptoms such as anxiety, flashbacks, and a sense of helplessness.

Chronic Trauma: Unlike acute trauma, chronic trauma stems from repeated and prolonged exposure to distressing situations. This can include ongoing abuse, neglect, or living in a war-torn area. The key characteristic of chronic trauma is that it wears down the individual over time. The repeated nature of these experiences can lead to a sense of hopelessness, emotional numbness, and a feeling that the traumatic situation is never-ending.

Complex Trauma: Complex trauma involves exposure to multiple, varied traumatic events, often of an invasive, interpersonal nature. This can include long-term domestic violence, childhood abuse, or being in a manipulative relationship. The combination of multiple traumas over time can deeply affect one's sense of self, leading to issues such as difficulty with emotional regulation, trust issues, and a distorted self-image.

Each type of trauma affects us differently, but they all share a common thread: they shake the foundation of who we are and how we see the world. Trauma isn't just about what happened; it's about how those events changed us. They leave an overwhelming wave that crashes over us, leaving us struggling to catch our breath.

For me, the trauma wasn't just the sadness of loss; it was the stress of having to navigate adulthood and caretaking at a young age. The impact wasn't limited to my emotional state; it seeped into my physical health, relationships, and daily life. The effects of trauma can be pervasive, altering the way we think, feel, and interact with the world around us.

The Ripple Effects of Trauma

Trauma doesn't just disappear after the event. It has rippling effects that touch every part of our lives. When trauma occurs, it's like dropping a stone into a pond—its effects spread out in waves, affecting every part of our being. These effects can be emotional, physical, psychological, and spiritual.

After my mum passed away, I experienced a range of emotions—shock, anger, guilt, and confusion. These feelings weren't just fleeting; they influenced my behavior, my decisions, and even how I saw myself. The trauma didn't just affect me in the immediate aftermath of the event; it continued to shape my life in profound ways long after the initial shock had passed.

Emotionally, I was often overwhelmed. I struggled to make sense of my feelings, and there were days when I felt completely numb, as if I were just going through the motions. The weight of grief and responsibility bore down on me, making it difficult to enjoy anything or find meaning in daily activities.

In the months and years following the loss, I struggled with a sense of inadequacy and self-doubt. I questioned my ability to take care of my siblings and often felt overwhelmed by the responsibilities that were suddenly mine. These feelings of inadequacy weren't just about the tasks at hand; they seeped into my overall sense of self-worth, making me feel like I wasn't good enough in any area of my life.

My emotional state affected my relationships with others, making it difficult to connect with friends who couldn't fully understand my situation. I withdrew from social activities and found it hard to relate to people who hadn't experienced similar losses. This isolation only deepened my sense of loneliness and despair.

Trauma also has a way of affecting our sense of safety and trust. For me, the sudden loss of my mum left me feeling insecure and anxious about the future. The stability I had taken for granted was gone, and I was left trying to build a new sense of security from the ground up. This anxiety wasn't just about my immediate circumstances; it became a constant undercurrent in my life, affecting everything from my ability to make decisions to my willingness to take risks.

The Importance of Acknowledging Trauma

One of the first steps in healing is acknowledging that trauma has occurred and that it's affecting you. This might seem obvious, but it's often the hardest step to take. It's easy to dismiss our experiences or try to "push through" without addressing the underlying pain. We live in a society that often encourages us to be strong, to "move on," and to avoid dwelling on the past. But when it comes to trauma, this approach can do more harm than good.

Acknowledging trauma is about more than just admitting that something bad happened. It's about recognizing the full impact of that event on your life—emotionally, physically, and mentally. It's about understanding that your feelings and reactions are valid, even if others don't see or understand them.

By acknowledging what you've been through, you give yourself permission to feel and heal. It's about validating your own experiences and understanding that your feelings and reactions are legitimate. This acknowledgment is the first step in reclaiming your sense of self and beginning the journey towards healing.

For me, acknowledging my trauma meant allowing myself to grieve—not just for my mum but also for the life I lost when she passed away. It meant recognizing that the weight I felt on my shoulders wasn't just a sign of weakness or failure; it was a natural response to an incredibly difficult situation.

Acknowledging trauma also means being honest with yourself about the ways it has affected you. This can be painful, but it's necessary for healing. It's okay to admit that you're struggling, that you're not okay, and that you need help. In fact, this is a sign of strength, not weakness.

When you acknowledge your trauma, you open the door to healing. You allow yourself to start processing the pain, to seek out support, and to take steps towards recovery. This might involve talking to a therapist, joining a support group, or simply allowing yourself to feel the emotions you've been suppressing. Whatever it looks like for you, the important thing is that you take that first step.

Moving Beyond Stigma and Misunderstanding

There can be a lot of stigma and misunderstanding around trauma. Some people might view it as a sign of weakness or think that you should just "get over it." Others might minimize your experiences, suggesting that "things could be worse" or that you're "overreacting." These attitudes can be incredibly damaging and make it harder to seek help or even acknowledge your trauma in the first place.

It's important to challenge these misconceptions and understand that trauma is a serious and valid experience. Trauma is not a sign of weakness; it's a response to overwhelming events. It doesn't matter how strong or resilient you are—everyone has a breaking point. When you reach that point, it's not a reflection of your character or worth; it's a natural, human response to extreme stress.

Healing from trauma is a courageous act, and seeking help or taking steps to address your experiences is a testament to your strength and resilience. It takes tremendous courage to face your pain head-on, to confront the memories and emotions you'd rather forget, and to do the hard work of healing. But it's also one of the most powerful things you can do for yourself.

The Science of Trauma

Before we dive deep, let's learn the science behind trauma—a topic that can feel both fascinating and overwhelming. Understanding how trauma impacts our brain and body is crucial because it helps us make sense of our experiences and guides us on the path to healing. Let's learn the intricate workings of our brain and body to uncover how trauma affects us at a fundamental level.

The Brain on Trauma: How Our Minds Respond

Our brain is a remarkable organ, responsible for our thoughts, emotions, and physical responses. Trauma affects various parts of the brain, each playing a unique role in how we experience and process stress. Understanding these mechanisms can shed light on why trauma has such a profound impact on our mental and physical well-being.

The Limbic System: Our Emotional Center

The limbic system is often referred to as the brain's emotional center, playing a critical role in how we process emotions and store memories. It includes key structures like the amygdala and hippocampus, which work together to help us navigate our emotional experiences and remember significant events.

The Amygdala: The amygdala is the brain's alarm system, responsible for detecting threats and triggering our fight-or-flight response. When we encounter a stressful or traumatic event, the amygdala springs into action, flooding our body with stress hormones like adrenaline. This reaction is designed to protect us from danger by heightening our awareness and preparing us to respond quickly.

However, when trauma occurs, the amygdala can become hyperactive, constantly scanning for threats even when none exist. This heightened sensitivity can lead to a state of chronic anxiety or fear, where everyday situations feel overwhelming or unsafe. It's as if the brain gets stuck in survival mode, making it difficult to relax or feel secure.

The Hippocampus: The hippocampus, another key player in the limbic system, is essential for processing and storing memories. It helps us distinguish between past and present experiences and allows us to recall information when needed. However, trauma can disrupt the functioning of the hippocampus, making it difficult to differentiate between what happened in the past and what is happening now.

This disruption can result in flashbacks or intrusive memories, where the traumatic event feels like it is happening all over again. Additionally, trauma can impair the hippocampus's ability to create coherent memories, leading to fragmented or disjointed recollections of the event. This confusion can add to the emotional turmoil, making it harder to process and heal from the trauma.

The Prefrontal Cortex: Our Decision-Maker

The prefrontal cortex is the brain's executive center, responsible for higher-order thinking, decision-making, and impulse control. It helps us plan, organize, and regulate our emotions, allowing us to respond to situations thoughtfully rather than reactively.

Stress and the Prefrontal Cortex: Under normal circumstances, the prefrontal cortex helps us navigate complex decisions and maintain self-control. However, when we are under extreme stress or experiencing trauma, this part of the brain can become less active. The flood of stress hormones, like cortisol, can impair the prefrontal cortex's ability to function optimally.

As a result, we might find ourselves reacting impulsively, struggling to concentrate, or having difficulty planning and organizing our thoughts. This can lead to feelings of being overwhelmed or out of control, as our ability to manage emotions and make rational decisions is compromised. The reduction in prefrontal cortex activity can make it challenging to think clearly, which can exacerbate the sense of helplessness often associated with trauma.

The HPA Axis: Our Stress Response System

The hypothalamic-pituitary-adrenal (HPA) axis is a critical component of our body's stress response system. It regulates the release of cortisol, a hormone that helps us manage stress by increasing energy levels and focus during threatening situations.

Short-Term vs. Long-Term Effects of Cortisol

In the short term, the activation of the HPA axis is beneficial. It prepares our body to handle immediate stressors by mobilizing energy reserves, increasing alertness, and enhancing our ability to respond to danger. However, when the HPA axis remains activated over extended periods, as often happens with chronic stress or trauma, the prolonged production of cortisol can have detrimental effects on the body.

Elevated cortisol levels can lead to a variety of health issues, including fatigue, weight gain, and difficulty managing stress. Over time, the constant state of heightened stress can strain other systems in the body, making it harder to recover from stressors and maintain overall well-being. This chronic stress response can leave us feeling drained, both physically and emotionally, and more vulnerable to further stressors.

The Body's Response to Trauma: The Physical Impact

Trauma doesn't just affect our minds; it also has significant effects on our bodies. The physical manifestations of trauma can be profound, influencing various aspects of our health and well-being. Understanding how trauma impacts the body is essential for a holistic approach to healing.

The Fight-or-Flight Response

The "fight-or-flight" response is our body's natural reaction to perceived danger. When we encounter a threat, our bodies release adrenaline and other stress hormones to prepare us to either confront the threat or escape from it. This response includes increased heart rate, heightened senses, and a surge of energy.

While this response is crucial for handling immediate danger, prolonged exposure to trauma can keep our bodies in a constant state of readiness.

Chronic Stress and Its Effects

Extended exposure to trauma and stress can have a variety of long-term effects on the body. Chronic stress impacts nearly every system in the body, leading to both physical and emotional health challenges.

Digestive Issues: The digestive system is particularly sensitive to stress. When we are stressed, the body's focus shifts away from digestion, leading to problems such as stomachaches, nausea, changes in appetite, or digestive disorders like irritable bowel syndrome (IBS). Over time, chronic stress can disrupt the balance of the gut, affecting everything from nutrient absorption to gut flora, and can lead to long-term digestive issues.

Cardiovascular Problems: Prolonged stress puts a strain on the cardiovascular system, increasing the risk of hypertension (high blood pressure), heart disease, and other cardiovascular issues. The constant release of stress hormones like cortisol and adrenaline can cause the heart to work harder, leading to long-term damage to the heart and blood vessels.

Sleep Disturbances: Trauma-related stress often results in sleep issues such as insomnia, nightmares, or fragmented sleep. Poor sleep can further exacerbate feelings of stress and anxiety, creating a cycle of discomfort. The lack of restorative sleep can impair the body's ability to heal and regenerate, making it even more challenging to recover from trauma.

Muscle Tension: Persistent stress can cause muscles to remain in a contracted state, leading to chronic pain, headaches, and back problems. This muscle tension can be a physical reminder of ongoing stress and trauma, contributing to a sense of discomfort and unease. The body's constant state of tension can also lead to issues such as migraines and tension headaches, further affecting quality of life.

Immune System Impact

The immune system is designed to protect the body from infections and diseases. However, chronic stress and trauma can weaken this system, making us more susceptible to illnesses and slowing down recovery processes.

Stress and Immune Function

Stress hormones like cortisol can suppress immune function, reducing the body's ability to fight off infections and repair damaged tissues. This suppression can leave us more vulnerable to illnesses and slow down the healing process. Over time, a weakened immune system can lead to more frequent illnesses and a longer recovery time from injuries or infections.

The impact of chronic stress on the immune system is significant, as it not only makes us more susceptible to common illnesses like colds and flu but can also exacerbate existing health conditions. Chronic inflammation, often linked to stress, has been associated with a range of health problems, including autoimmune disorders, cardiovascular diseases, and more.

The Connection Between Mind and Body

The relationship between the mind and body is intricate and profound. What happens in our brains can significantly affect our physical health, and vice versa. Understanding this connection can be both enlightening and empowering as you work through your healing journey.

Emotional Stress and Physical Pain

Emotional stress from trauma can manifest as physical pain. For example, the tension and anxiety that come from trauma can lead to headaches, back pain, and other discomforts. This physical pain is not just a byproduct of stress but a reflection of how deeply intertwined our emotional and physical states are.

The Mind-Body Connection

When we experience emotional distress, our body often responds in kind. Tension in the mind can translate into tension in the muscles, leading to pain and discomfort. This connection highlights the importance of addressing both emotional and physical health in the healing process. For instance, practices like mindfulness, meditation, and relaxation techniques can help alleviate both emotional and physical symptoms by calming the mind and relaxing the body.

Somatization

Somatization is the process by which emotional distress is expressed through physical symptoms. This can include unexplained aches and pains, gastrointestinal issues, and other physical symptoms that have no clear medical cause. Understanding somatization is crucial in recognizing how trauma can affect not just the mind but the entire body.

Mental Health and Physical Health

Mental health conditions like anxiety and depression, which are often rooted in trauma, can also have physical effects. Chronic stress and emotional strain can lead to fatigue, changes in appetite, and general physical malaise. Addressing mental health is essential not just for emotional well-being but for overall physical health as well.

The Physical Manifestations of Mental Health Issues

Anxiety and depression can lead to a range of physical

symptoms, including fatigue, changes in appetite, and chronic pain. These symptoms can create a feedback loop, where physical discomfort exacerbates emotional distress, and vice versa. For example, a person experiencing chronic pain may feel more anxious or depressed, while someone struggling with anxiety may find themselves feeling physically unwell.

The Importance of Holistic Healing

Healing from trauma requires a holistic approach that addresses both mental and physical health. This means recognizing the ways in which emotional distress can manifest in the body and seeking treatments that support both aspects of well-being. Techniques such as therapy, physical exercise, proper nutrition, and stress management can all play a role in helping individuals recover from trauma and restore their overall health.

Understanding how trauma affects both the brain and body provides a comprehensive view of its impact. It underscores the importance of addressing both aspects in the healing process. By recognizing the physical and emotional effects of trauma, you can better navigate your journey toward recovery.

Deep Dive into The Fight, Flight, or Freeze Response

The Fight, Flight, or Freeze Response is a fundamental part of our stress response system: the fight, flight, or freeze response.

It's a term you might have heard before, but understanding it deeply can be incredibly empowering. This response is a natural part of our biology, designed to protect us in moments of danger. However, when it's triggered frequently or inappropriately, it can affect our daily lives and well-being.

The Basics of the Fight, Flight, or Freeze Response

The fight, flight, or freeze response is one of the body's most primal survival mechanisms, designed to protect us from harm. It's an automatic reaction, deeply embedded in our biology, and part of the autonomic nervous system—which controls involuntary functions like heart rate, digestion, and breathing. This response is triggered when we perceive a threat, real or imagined, and it readies our body to either face the danger, escape from it, or become momentarily immobilized. Understanding this response is key to comprehending how trauma affects us and how we can begin to manage its impact.

Fight: When the body decides that confronting the threat is the best option, it enters the fight mode. This is marked by a surge of adrenaline, which increases your heart rate, dilates your pupils, and directs blood flow to your muscles. The goal is to prepare you for physical confrontation, giving you the strength and energy to fend off the perceived danger. This response might manifest as sudden anger, irritability, or aggression, even in situations where such reactions may not be warranted.

Flight: The flight response is the body's way of preparing to flee from danger. When this mode is activated, your body becomes hyper-alert, and your senses become more acute. You might feel an overwhelming urge to escape, and your body will redirect its resources toward getting you out of the situation as quickly as possible. This might include an increased heart rate, shallow breathing, and a rush of adrenaline. In everyday life, the flight response might appear as avoidance, such as steering clear of places or people that remind you of past trauma.

Freeze: Sometimes, when faced with overwhelming danger, the body's response is to freeze. This can be seen as the body's attempt to avoid detection or to play dead. During a freeze response, you might feel paralyzed, unable to move or think clearly. Your body might shut down to a certain degree, as if waiting for the threat to pass. In some cases, people might dissociate, mentally disconnecting from the reality of the situation to protect themselves from the trauma. This response can be particularly frustrating, as it often leaves you feeling powerless and trapped in the moment.

Navigating the Fight, Flight, or Freeze Response

Understanding your body's natural response to stress is the first step in learning how to manage it. While the fight, flight, or freeze response is a necessary survival mechanism, it can be triggered in situations where the threat is not life-threatening, leading to unnecessary stress and anxiety. Recognizing what triggers these responses and developing strategies to manage them can help you regain control and respond more effectively in stressful situations.

Recognizing Triggers

Triggers are stimuli that activate the fight, flight, or freeze response. They can be external, like a particular place, sound, or smell, or internal, like a memory or emotion. Identifying your triggers is crucial for managing your stress response. Here are some common types of triggers:

Stressful Situations: High-pressure environments, conflicts, or looming deadlines can easily trigger a fight, flight, or freeze response. Your body perceives these situations as threats, and it reacts accordingly, even if the actual danger is not physical.

Past Trauma: Trauma leaves a deep imprint on the mind and body. Memories of past traumatic events can trigger your survival response, often leading to feelings of panic or anxiety. These memories don't always have to be conscious; sometimes, they're buried deep within the subconscious, and a seemingly unrelated event can bring them to the surface.

Internal Triggers: Sometimes, it's not an external event but rather your own thoughts and feelings that trigger the response. Negative self-talk, overwhelming emotions, or even physical sensations like a racing heart can set off the fight, flight, or freeze response.

By becoming more aware of your triggers, you can start to anticipate them and take steps to manage your reactions.

Techniques for Managing the Response

Once you've identified your triggers, the next step is learning how to manage the fight, flight, or freeze response. Here are some practical strategies:

Deep Breathing: One of the simplest yet most effective ways to calm your nervous system is through deep breathing. When you take slow, deep breaths, you activate the parasympathetic nervous system, which counteracts the fight, flight, or freeze response. Try inhaling deeply through your nose, holding your breath for a few seconds, and then exhaling slowly through your mouth. This practice can help you regain control over your body and reduce the intensity of the response.

Grounding Techniques: Grounding exercises are designed to help you stay present and focused in the moment, reducing feelings of being overwhelmed. One common technique is the 5-4-3-2-1 method: Identify five things you can see, four things you can touch, three things you can hear, two things you can smell, and one thing you can taste. This exercise engages your senses and helps pull you out of the fight, flight, or freeze state.

Physical Activity: Regular exercise is an excellent way to regulate your body's stress response system. Physical activity helps release built-up tension and promotes the release of endorphins, which are natural stress relievers. Even a short walk, gentle stretching, or yoga can make a significant difference in how you manage stress.

Relaxation Techniques: Techniques such as progressive muscle relaxation, meditation, or yoga can help you release physical tension and calm your mind. Progressive muscle relaxation involves tensing and then slowly relaxing each muscle group in your body, starting from your toes and working your way up to your head. This practice can help reduce the physical symptoms of the fight, flight, or freeze response.

Seeking Support: Sometimes, managing the fight, flight, or freeze response requires more than just self-help strategies. Seeking support from a therapist or counselor can provide you with valuable tools and insights into your stress responses. Therapy can help you understand the root causes of your triggers and develop personalized strategies for managing them.

Embracing Healing

The fight, flight, or freeze response is a natural part of being human, but it doesn't have to control your life. By recognizing your triggers and developing strategies to manage your responses, you can begin to reclaim your sense of peace and stability.

Healing from trauma involves more than just managing stress—it's about embracing the journey toward wholeness. This journey includes acknowledging the impact that trauma has had on your body and mind, and taking proactive steps to nurture your well-being. As you build resilience and learn to respond to stress in healthier ways, you'll find that you're not just surviving, but thriving.

The path to healing is deeply personal and can be challenging, but it is also filled with opportunities for growth and self-discovery. By understanding the fight, flight, or freeze response and learning how to manage it, you're taking important steps toward a more peaceful, balanced, and fulfilling life.

Relating Science to Personal Experience

I'd like to bridge the gap between the scientific concepts of trauma and the very real experiences that many of us go through. Understanding the science behind trauma can be incredibly enlightening, but it's the personal connection that truly brings these concepts to life. I want to share how these scientific principles resonate with my own journey, particularly the overwhelming stress and responsibility I felt after losing my mum.

The Overwhelming Stress of Trauma

The Science Behind Stress

We've talked about the fight, flight, or freeze response and how it's activated by the brain in times of perceived danger. This response triggers a cascade of physiological changes: increased heart rate, heightened senses, and a surge of energy, all designed to help us deal with immediate threats.

But what happens when this response is triggered not just occasionally but as a constant state? That's where chronic stress comes into play. The constant activation of the HPA (hypothalamic-pituitary-adrenal) axis leads to sustained high levels of cortisol, the stress hormone. This chronic stress impacts nearly every system in our body, leading to both physical and emotional challenges.

My Experience: A Surge of Stress

The loss of my mum at 17 was a life-altering event that catapulted me into a role I was unprepared for. Suddenly, I was not only grieving but also responsible for taking care of my younger siblings and managing the household. This overwhelming burden triggered my stress response in a way I had never experienced before.

I remember feeling like I was constantly on high alert, my heart racing with even the slightest challenge. The smallest tasks seemed insurmountable, and the weight of responsibility was almost unbearable. My body felt like it was in a perpetual state of fight or flight, reacting to every new challenge as if it were a life-or-death situation. The relentless stress was exhausting, leaving me physically and emotionally drained.

The Burden of Responsibility: The Psychological Impact

The Cognitive Load of Trauma

Trauma doesn't just impact us physically; it also affects our cognitive processes. The constant state of stress can impair our decision-making abilities and our capacity to think clearly. The prefrontal cortex, which is responsible for higher-order thinking, becomes less active under stress.

This can lead to difficulties with concentration, memory, and decision-making. It's a challenging cognitive load to bear, as you're constantly trying to navigate an overwhelming situation with a mind that feels like it's functioning at less than full capacity.

My Experience: Navigating Daily Challenges

During the time after my mum's passing, I often felt like my brain was stuck in a loop of worry and fear. Decisions that should have been straightforward felt monumental, and I struggled to maintain focus on my studies and responsibilities. The cognitive burden of managing the household, taking care of my siblings, and trying to keep up with schoolwork was intense.

I found myself forgetting important things—missing deadlines, appointments, and even basic tasks. My mind was so consumed with the weight of my responsibilities that it felt like I was constantly operating in a fog. It was as if my brain was overwhelmed, and I was just trying to survive each day, one task at a time. The mental exhaustion made it difficult to find clarity or peace in any aspect of my life.

The Physical Toll: From Muscle Tension to Health Issues

Physical Symptoms of Chronic Stress

The physiological impact of chronic stress is profound. Prolonged activation of the fight-or-flight response can lead to various physical symptoms like muscle tension. Sleep disturbance and digestive issues.

My Experience: A Body Out of Sync

The constant stress I was under began to manifest in my body in ways I couldn't ignore. The tension in my shoulders and neck became chronic, leading to debilitating headaches that made it difficult to function. My once-resilient body started to feel like it was rebelling against me.

Sleep became elusive. I would lie awake at night, my mind racing with worries and a never-ending to-do list. Despite spending hours in bed, I would wake up feeling exhausted, as though I hadn't slept at all. Mornings were particularly tough, and it felt like I was starting each day on the back foot.

My digestive system also started to suffer. There were days when I felt nauseous, and other times when my appetite would disappear completely. It was as if my body was protesting the unrelenting stress I was under, signaling that something needed to change. The physical toll of stress was a constant reminder of the emotional burden I was carrying.

The Emotional Strain: Navigating Feelings of Overwhelm

Emotional Impact of Trauma

Trauma takes a significant emotional toll, affecting our mood, outlook on life, and overall emotional well-being. The constant state of stress can lead to feelings of sadness, anxiety, and overwhelm, often resulting in emotional exhaustion. This emotional strain can make it difficult to cope with everyday challenges, leading to a sense of being constantly drained and depleted.

My Experience: A Rollercoaster of Emotions

Emotionally, I felt like I was on a never-ending rollercoaster. The grief of losing my mum was overwhelming, and the added responsibility of caring for my siblings only intensified these emotions. There were days when the sadness was so profound that it felt like I was drowning in it, and other times when anxiety would grip me, leaving me paralyzed with worry about how I was going to manage everything.

Despite my efforts to stay strong for my siblings, I often felt like I was barely holding it together. My emotions were raw and unpredictable, making it difficult to maintain any sense of normalcy. It was a constant struggle to balance my own grief and anxiety with the need to be there for my family. The emotional strain was immense, and it often felt like I was fighting a battle on multiple fronts, with no clear end in sight.

Recognizing Trauma in Your Life

In our journey towards healing, one of the crucial steps is recognizing trauma in our lives. It's not always easy to spot, especially when it blends into our daily routines and becomes a part of our normal. But understanding the signs and symptoms can be incredibly empowering. It's the first step towards acknowledging and addressing the impact trauma has had on our lives.

I want to share my experiences with you—how I came to recognize trauma in my own life, and how you might see these signs in yours.

Emotional Symptoms: The Invisible Burden

Persistent Sadness and Depression

Trauma often leaves behind a deep emotional imprint that manifests as persistent sadness or depression. This isn't the typical sadness that comes and goes with daily ups and downs. Instead, it's a profound, lingering feeling that seems to settle into your bones, making it hard to find joy or interest in activities you once loved. You may find yourself withdrawing from social interactions, losing interest in hobbies, and feeling a pervasive sense of hopelessness. This kind of sadness is not just an emotional response but a clear indicator that something deeper is at play.

My Experience: The Shadows of Sadness

After my mum passed away, the sadness I felt wasn't just a fleeting emotion—it was a deep, consuming sorrow that colored every aspect of my life. Activities that once brought me joy, like spending time with friends or pursuing my favorite hobbies, suddenly felt hollow and meaningless. I found myself withdrawing from social interactions, not because I wanted to be alone, but because I simply didn't have the energy or the will to engage. It felt like a shadow had been cast over my entire existence, and recognizing this as a symptom of trauma was a crucial step in understanding the depth of my emotional wounds.

Heightened Anxiety and Fear

Trauma doesn't just affect our emotions; it can also heighten our sense of anxiety and fear. You might find yourself constantly on edge, feeling a sense of dread even when there's no immediate threat. This heightened state of alert can be both exhausting and overwhelming, leading to a constant feeling of being on the brink of something going wrong. It's as if your mind and body are perpetually in "fight or flight" mode, unable to relax or find peace.

My Experience: Living on the Edge of Anxiety

In the months following my mum's death, I lived in a state of constant anxiety. Simple, everyday tasks like going to the grocery store or managing household chores suddenly felt overwhelming and fraught with potential disasters. I was always on edge, worrying about what might go wrong next. This constant fear wasn't just draining—it was debilitating. It impacted every aspect of my life, from my relationships to my ability to function at school. Recognizing this anxiety as a symptom of trauma was the first step toward seeking support and finding strategies to manage my fear

Physical Symptoms: The Body's Response

Trauma doesn't just weigh on our minds; it takes a toll on our bodies as well. One of the most common physical symptoms of trauma is chronic fatigue, where no amount of sleep seems to be enough. You might also experience sleep disturbances like insomnia, where falling asleep or staying asleep becomes a nightly battle. This relentless exhaustion isn't just about being tired—it's your body's way of telling you that it's under significant stress and needs help.

My Experience: The Exhaustion That Sleep Couldn't Cure

The emotional toll of losing my mum and taking on new responsibilities manifested physically as chronic exhaustion. No matter how much I slept, I always felt like I was running on empty. Nights became battles with insomnia, where my mind raced with worries and responsibilities, making it impossible to rest. The exhaustion was more than just physical—it was mental and emotional, a sign that my body and mind were struggling to cope with the trauma I was experiencing.

Unexplained Aches and Pains

Trauma often manifests as physical symptoms that seem to have no clear cause. You might experience unexplained aches and pains, particularly in your muscles and joints. Common areas include the neck, shoulders, and back, where tension often settles. Digestive issues, such as stomachaches, nausea, or changes in appetite, can also arise, making it clear that trauma impacts not just the mind but the body as well.

My Experience

I experienced constant muscle tension, particularly in my neck and shoulders. These physical symptoms were my body's way of expressing the stress and trauma I was under. The tension often led to debilitating headaches, making it hard to focus on anything else. My digestive system also became unpredictable, with nausea and a lack of appetite becoming common occurrences. These physical symptoms were my body's cry for help, a clear signal that the trauma I was experiencing was affecting me on every level.

Behavioral Symptoms: Changes in Daily Life

Withdrawal from Social Activities: Retreating into Isolation

One of the behavioral symptoms of trauma is a withdrawal from social activities and relationships. You might find yourself avoiding gatherings, declining invitations, or simply not reaching out to friends and family as you once did. This isolation isn't just about wanting to be alone—it's often a way to protect yourself from the overwhelming emotions that social interactions can bring up. However, this retreat into solitude can deepen feelings of loneliness and make it harder to reconnect with others later on.

My Experience: The Comfort of Solitude and the Pain of Isolation

I found myself retreating into solitude. Social activities that I once enjoyed became overwhelming, and I began to avoid gatherings and interactions. It felt safer to stay at home, away from the emotional demands of socializing. But this withdrawal also deepened my sense of isolation, making it harder to reach out when I needed support. Recognizing this behavior as a symptom of trauma was important in understanding my need for connection and support.

How Trauma Manifests in Relationships, Self-Esteem, and Everyday Life

An important aspect of trauma—how it seeps into various facets of our lives, including our relationships, self-esteem, and daily routines. Understanding these manifestations can offer profound insights into our healing journey. I want to share how trauma played out in my own life, with the hope that it resonates with your experiences and helps you navigate your path to healing.

Trauma and Relationships: The Ripple Effect

Strained Relationships

Trauma can deeply affect how we interact with others. For me, the loss of my mum and the subsequent responsibilities I took on created strains in my relationships. I found myself withdrawing from friends and family, not because I didn't care, but because I was overwhelmed and emotionally drained.

In the aftermath of mum's death, I felt isolated even when surrounded by people. The emotional weight of my new responsibilities made it challenging to connect authentically with those around me. I often felt misunderstood, and my friends and family struggled to comprehend the depth of my grief and stress. This led to misunderstandings and communication breakdowns.

I also became more irritable and less patient. Simple disagreements felt magnified, and my responses were often colored by my inner turmoil. I would snap at loved ones or withdraw into myself, creating a barrier that made it difficult for them to reach out and offer support.

Difficulty Trusting Others

Trauma can affect our ability to trust, which can be particularly challenging in relationships. For me, the betrayal of losing my mum and the sudden shift in my responsibilities made it hard to trust others fully. I worried that people might let me down or that they wouldn't understand my situation.

I became guarded and found it hard to let people in. I feared vulnerability, believing that if I opened up, I might be judged or dismissed. This guardedness created a barrier between me and others, making it difficult to build and maintain meaningful connections.

Recognizing this tendency was a crucial step in understanding how trauma was affecting my relationships. It helped me work on opening up and rebuilding trust, both with myself and others.

Trauma and Self-Esteem: The Inner Struggle

Erosion of Self-Worth

Trauma can erode our sense of self-worth, making us question our value and capabilities. For me, the overwhelming responsibilities and emotional burden led to a diminished sense of self-esteem. I often felt inadequate and wondered if I was doing enough or if I was enough.

As I juggled the demands of caring for my siblings and managing my own grief, self-doubt crept in. I questioned whether I was handling things well or if I was failing my family. This constant self-criticism made it hard to see my own strengths and achievements.

I compared myself to others who seemed to be handling their lives effortlessly, which only deepened my feelings of inadequacy. Recognizing these patterns of self-doubt and harsh self-criticism was a key part of my healing process.

Impaired Self-Care

Trauma can also impact how we take care of ourselves. In the midst of managing my responsibilities, I often neglected my own needs. Self-care became a distant concept as I focused on meeting the needs of others and managing daily life.

I frequently put my own needs on the back burner. Whether it was skipping meals, neglecting exercise, or ignoring my emotional needs, self-care felt like a luxury I couldn't afford. This neglect took a toll on my overall well-being, making it clear that addressing self-esteem and self-care was vital for my healing.

Difficulty Finding Joy

Trauma can diminish our ability to find joy and pleasure in daily activities. For me, the emotional burden made it hard to appreciate simple pleasures. Activities that once brought me joy, like spending time with friends or enjoying a hobby, felt hollow.

I found it challenging to feel genuine happiness. Even when surrounded by moments of joy or opportunities for fun, it often felt like there was a cloud of sadness overshadowing these experiences. Recognizing this as a symptom of trauma helped me understand why finding joy felt elusive and motivated me to seek ways to reconnect with positive experiences.

Reflect On Your Own Experiences and Recognize Trauma in Your Life

As we journey through understanding trauma, I want to take a moment to encourage you to reflect deeply on your own experiences. Recognizing trauma in your life is a profound act of self-awareness, one that opens the door to healing and transformation. It's not always easy to look back and confront the moments that have caused us pain, but this is where true healing begins. By acknowledging the wounds of the past, you're taking an incredibly courageous step—one that not only honors your past but also empowers your future.

This process of reflection is holding up a mirror to your soul. It allows you to see where you've been, how far you've come, and where you still need to go. It's an invitation to understand yourself more fully, to uncover the layers of hurt that might still be affecting you today. And as you do this, remember to be gentle with yourself. Healing is not a race; it's a journey that unfolds at its own pace.

Every time you allow yourself to sit with your emotions, to truly feel them and understand them, you're taking a vital step forward. This is not about reliving the pain, but about reclaiming your power over it. It's about saying, "This happened to me, and it was hard. But I am here, and I am healing."

Know that you're not alone in this journey. Many have walked this path before, and many are walking it now. It's a path that, though difficult, leads to greater self-compassion, resilience, and ultimately, peace. So, as you reflect, do so with kindness toward yourself. Celebrate the strength it takes to even consider this process. Recognize that in this moment, by simply acknowledging your trauma, you're already moving toward healing.

You're taking one of the most important steps you can take for your well-being. You're showing yourself the love and care that you deserve. Keep going—each reflection, each moment of awareness, is a step closer to the peace and healing that you seek.

The Journey to Healing

The Decision to Heal

There comes a moment in life when you realize that carrying the weight of your past is no longer an option. It's a moment that isn't always marked by a grand revelation or a dramatic change. Sometimes, it's a quiet whisper in your heart, a soft nudge that tells you, "It's time." For me, that moment came when I realized that the pain I was holding onto was not just a part of my past but was bleeding into every part of my present.

For years, I pushed through. I held it all together because I believed that was what I was supposed to do. I buried my feelings deep inside, convincing myself that if I could just keep moving forward, everything would eventually be okay. But as the years went by, the pain didn't disappear. It lingered, quietly festering beneath the surface, showing up in ways I didn't even recognize at the time. It manifested in my relationships, my self-esteem, and my ability to trust others. I became so accustomed to the pain that it started to feel like a part of me—a part I couldn't imagine living without.

Then, one day, I reached a point where I couldn't carry it anymore. It wasn't a sudden breakdown or a dramatic event that brought me to this place. It was more like a slow, steady realization that I was tired—tired of pretending everything was okay, tired of carrying this invisible burden that was suffocating me from the inside out. I looked at my life and saw how much the trauma was holding me back, how it was preventing me from living fully, from loving deeply, from embracing the person I was meant to be.

I remember sitting alone in my room, the house quiet except for the distant hum of life happening outside my window. I felt a heaviness in my chest, a physical weight that had been there for as long as I could remember. And in that moment, something shifted. I realized that I didn't want to live like this anymore. I didn't want my mum's death to define me, to be the lens through which I viewed the world. I wanted to honor her memory by living a life that was full, vibrant, and free from the chains of my past.

That was the moment I decided to heal. It wasn't a decision made lightly, nor was it one I fully understood at the time. But I knew that I couldn't continue down the path I was on. I had to make a change, and that change had to start with me. It was the beginning of a journey that would take me through the darkest corners of my soul, but it was also the first step toward reclaiming my life.

Healing, I soon learned, is not a linear process. It's messy and unpredictable, full of ups and downs, setbacks and breakthroughs. There were days when I felt like I was making progress, and then there were days when it seemed like I was right back where I started. But each time I faltered, I reminded myself of that moment in my room, of the decision I made to choose healing over suffering.

One of the most important things I realized during this journey was that healing is a choice we have to make every single day. It's not a one-time decision; it's a commitment to ourselves, to our well-being, and to our future. It's about choosing to face the pain, to sit with it, and to work through it rather than letting it control our lives. It's about recognizing that while we can't change what happened to us, we do have the power to change how we respond to it.

The decision to heal meant allowing myself to grieve fully for the first time. It meant giving myself permission to feel the depth of my loss without trying to suppress it or push it away. I had to acknowledge the anger, the sadness, the fear—all the emotions I had buried so deep that I had almost forgotten they were there. It was a process of peeling back the layers, of uncovering the wounds that had never truly healed and giving them the attention they deserved.

I also had to learn to be kind to myself, to let go of the expectations I had placed on my shoulders. As the eldest daughter, I had always felt like I needed to be strong, to take care of everyone else, to keep it all together. But healing required me to be vulnerable, to admit that I didn't have all the answers, and that I needed help. It meant reaching out to others, finding support, and allowing myself to be held by those who cared about me.

The decision to heal also meant redefining what it meant to be strong. I realized that strength wasn't about pretending I was okay when I wasn't; it was about facing my pain head-on and working through it. It was about being honest with myself, acknowledging my feelings, and giving myself the space and time I needed to heal.

As I continued on this journey, I began to notice subtle changes in myself. I started to feel lighter, more at peace. The constant knot in my stomach began to loosen, and the fog that had clouded my mind for so long started to lift. It wasn't that the pain disappeared overnight, but it no longer consumed me the way it once had. I could breathe again, and for the first time in years, I felt a sense of hope for the future.

This journey of healing has been one of the most challenging experiences of my life, but it has also been one of the most rewarding. It has taught me that no matter how deep the pain, there is always a path to healing. It may not be easy, and it may take time, but it is possible. And it all starts with the decision to heal—to choose ourselves, to choose life, and to choose to move forward, one step at a time.

If you're reading this and you're at that crossroads, unsure of whether you can or should take that step, I want to encourage you. You are stronger than you know, and you deserve to live a life that is free from the shadows of your past. The decision to heal is one of the most powerful choices you can make for yourself. It's not about erasing the pain, but about transforming it into something that no longer holds you back. It's about finding peace, reclaiming your life, and embracing the person you are meant to be.

Take that first step. Make the decision to heal. Trust that the journey, as difficult as it may be, will lead you to a place of peace and freedom.

Overcoming fear and resistance to facing trauma

Facing trauma is standing at the edge of a deep, dark forest, knowing that the only way to find peace is to walk through it. It's natural to feel fear, to hesitate, and to wonder if you have the strength to make it to the other side. I know because I've been there too. The fear can be paralyzing, and the resistance to facing what's inside can feel almost insurmountable. But I want to tell you that even though that fear is real and valid, so too is the strength within you to overcome it.

When I first began to confront my own trauma, I was terrified. The idea of reopening wounds that had never fully healed was overwhelming. I had spent so much time trying to move past the pain, trying to bury it deep within so that I could carry on with life. I was afraid that if I allowed myself to truly face what I had been through, it would consume me. I was scared of the emotions I had kept bottled up for so long—of the grief, the anger, the guilt, and the sadness that I had tried so hard to push away.

But over time, I realized that avoiding the pain wasn't making it go away. It was simply lying dormant, waiting for moments of weakness to resurface in ways that I couldn't control. It was affecting my relationships, my self-esteem, and my ability to fully experience joy. The more I tried to ignore it, the more it influenced my life from the shadows. I had to come to terms with the fact that the only way out was through—that healing meant I had to face the very things I was so afraid of.

The resistance to facing trauma often comes from a place of self-preservation. Our minds and bodies are wired to protect us from pain, and when we've been through something traumatic, our instinct is to shield ourselves from experiencing that pain again. It's like touching a hot stove and pulling your hand back; our natural response is to avoid anything that might hurt us. But when it comes to trauma, this instinct can keep us trapped in a cycle of avoidance that prevents us from truly healing.

For me, the turning point came when I realized that I was tired of living in fear. I was tired of the way my trauma was holding me back, of how it was dictating my life without me even realizing it. I didn't want to be a prisoner of my past anymore. I wanted to break free, to reclaim my life, and to find the peace that I knew I deserved. But to do that, I had to overcome the fear and resistance that had been keeping me from facing the trauma head-on.

One of the first steps I took was acknowledging my fear. I allowed myself to feel it fully, to understand that it was a natural response to what I had been through. I didn't try to push it away or pretend it wasn't there. Instead, I sat with it, listened to it, and tried to understand where it was coming from. By acknowledging my fear, I was able to take some of its power away. It wasn't something to be ashamed of or to hide from—it was a part of my healing process.

Next, I began to break down the overwhelming task of facing my trauma into smaller, more manageable steps. I didn't have to confront everything all at once; I could take it one piece at a time. I started with the things that felt the least threatening and gradually worked my way up to the more difficult emotions and memories. This approach made the process feel less daunting and gave me a sense of control over my healing journey.

Another thing that helped me overcome the resistance was the realization that facing my trauma didn't mean reliving it. I had always been afraid that confronting my pain would mean reopening old wounds, that I would be dragged back into the darkness of those difficult times. But what I learned is that facing trauma is not about reliving it—it's about understanding it, processing it, and finding a way to move forward. It's about acknowledging what happened, recognizing how it affected you, and then finding a way to integrate that experience into your life in a way that allows you to heal.

I also found strength in the support of others. Opening up to trusted friends, family, or a therapist made a world of difference. It can be incredibly healing to share your story with someone who listens without judgment, who validates your feelings, and who helps you navigate the complexities of your emotions. Having a support system reminded me that I wasn't alone in my journey and that there were people who cared about my well-being. They offered perspectives that I hadn't considered and helped me see my own strength when I couldn't see it for myself.

Of course, there were setbacks along the way. There were days when the fear would resurface, when I would question whether I was strong enough to continue. But each time, I reminded myself of why I had started this journey in the first place. I reminded myself that I deserved to heal, that I deserved a life free from the shadows of my past. And each time I faced my fear and pushed through the resistance, I grew a little bit stronger, a little bit more confident in my ability to heal.

Overcoming fear and resistance is not about erasing those feelings—it's about acknowledging them, understanding them, and then choosing to move forward anyway. It's about recognizing that the path to healing is not always easy, but it is always worth it. It's about trusting that you have the strength within you to face whatever comes your way and that on the other side of that fear is a life filled with peace, joy, and freedom.

If you're struggling with fear and resistance on your own healing journey, It's okay and take your time. Healing is not a race; it's a personal journey that unfolds at your own pace. But I encourage you to take that first step, to face the fear and resistance with courage and compassion for yourself. Because on the other side of that fear lies the life you deserve—a life of peace, of wholeness, and of true, lasting healing.

Setting intentions for your own healing journey.

Setting intentions for your healing journey is very important. Each intention you set is a promise to yourself, a commitment to nurture your growth and to cultivate the life you want to live. When you take the time to set clear, heartfelt intentions, you're not just wishing for change—you're actively participating in your own transformation. It's a powerful step that sets the tone for everything that follows, guiding you through the ups and downs of the healing process.

When I first started my own healing journey, I didn't really understand the importance of setting intentions. I was so focused on just getting through each day that I didn't think much about what I wanted my life to look like on the other side of the pain. But as I moved forward, I realized that without clear intentions, I was like a ship without a rudder—just drifting, hoping to land somewhere better but not really steering my own course. Setting intentions changed that. It gave me direction, purpose, and a sense of control over my healing process.

So, how do you go about setting intentions for your healing journey? It starts with reflection—taking the time to really think about what you want and why it matters to you. This isn't about setting goals or making a to-do list; it's about connecting with your deepest desires and values. It's about asking yourself, "What do I want to heal? Why is this important to me? How do I want to feel? What kind of life do I want to create for myself?" These questions can guide you to the intentions that resonate most deeply with you.

When you're ready, find a quiet space where you can be alone with your thoughts. Grab a journal or a piece of paper, and start writing. Don't worry about getting it perfect or finding the right words—just let whatever comes to mind flow onto the page. Here are some prompts to help you get started:

What are the areas of my life where I feel most in need of healing? This could be related to relationships, self-esteem, past experiences, or even physical health. Think about where you feel the most pain or discomfort and let that guide your intentions.

How do I want to feel as I move through this healing process? Maybe you want to feel more at peace, more confident, or more connected to others. Whatever it is, write it down. Your feelings are an important part of your intentions.

What kind of person do I want to become as I heal? This is about envisioning your future self. Who are you becoming through this process? How do you want to show up in the world? What qualities do you want to cultivate within yourself?

What am I ready to let go of in order to heal? Healing often involves releasing things that no longer serve us—whether it's old beliefs, habits, or even relationships. Think about what you're ready to leave behind as you move forward.

What do I want to create in my life as I heal? This could be new opportunities, relationships, or ways of being. It's about looking ahead to the life you want to build on the foundation of your healing.

As you write, you might notice certain themes or desires that stand out to you. These are your intentions—your guiding stars on this journey. Once you've identified them, take a moment to sit with them. Read them over, feel their truth, and let them sink in. These intentions are your personal commitments to yourself, and they will be your anchor as you navigate the healing process.

It's important to remember that setting intentions is not a one-time event. As you move through your healing journey, your needs and desires might change. Your intentions should evolve with you. Revisit them regularly, check in with yourself, and don't be afraid to adjust them as needed. This process is fluid, just like healing itself. The more you stay connected to your intentions, the more they will support and guide you.

Another key part of setting intentions is to approach them with kindness and compassion toward yourself. Healing is a journey, not a destination, and it's okay if things don't go exactly as planned. Your intentions are there to guide you, not to pressure you. Be gentle with yourself, and remember that every step you take, no matter how small, is progress.

It can also be helpful to create a ritual around your intentions. This could be as simple as reading them aloud to yourself each morning, lighting a candle as you reflect on them, or even creating a vision board that visually represents your intentions. Rituals help to reinforce your commitments and keep your intentions at the forefront of your mind.

And finally, as you set your intentions, hold onto hope. Healing is a journey filled with challenges, but it is also filled with moments of profound growth, joy, and transformation. Your intentions are a testament to your strength and your desire for a better life. They are a reminder that you are not defined by your trauma, but by your resilience and your capacity to heal.

I encourage you to set your intentions with an open heart. Be honest with yourself about what you need and what you want. Trust that you have the strength to follow through on these intentions, even when the path gets difficult. And know that every step you take, no matter how small, is a step toward the life you are creating for yourself—a life filled with peace, joy, and healing.

As you move forward, keep your intentions close. Let them be your guide, your compass, and your source of strength. You are capable of incredible things, and your healing journey is just the beginning.

Seeking Support

One of the most crucial steps you can take in your healing journey is seeking support. Trauma doesn't have to be a solitary experience; in fact, healing often requires the strength, wisdom, and companionship of others. Whether through professional help, supportive friends, or community resources, reaching out for support can make a world of difference in your recovery.

Why Support Matters: The Power of Connection

Healing from trauma can be an overwhelming process, and it's easy to feel like you're facing it all on your own. However, seeking support is crucial because it allows you to share your burden with others who can offer empathy, understanding, and guidance. Connection with others helps to break the isolation that trauma often brings, and it reminds you that you're not alone in your struggles. Whether it's through talking about your experiences, receiving validation, or simply knowing that someone is there for you, support plays a vital role in the healing process.

The role of therapy and counseling in your healing process.

Therapy is one of the most courageous and transformative steps you can take on your healing journey. For many of us, asking for help doesn't come naturally. We're taught to be strong, to handle our problems on our own, and to keep going no matter what. But the truth is, healing is not something we're meant to do alone. It's a process that often requires the guidance, wisdom, and compassion of others. For me, seeking support was a pivotal moment in my healing process—a moment that changed everything.

Therapy and counseling became my lifeline during some of the darkest times of my life. After losing my mum, I was overwhelmed with grief, responsibility, and a deep sense of loss that I didn't know how to navigate. I tried to be strong for my siblings, to keep it all together, but inside, I was falling apart. It wasn't until I reached out for help that I began to understand the depth of my pain and the possibility of healing.

When I first started therapy, I wasn't sure what to expect. I had all sorts of preconceived notions about what it meant to see a therapist—fears about being judged, concerns about appearing weak, and a general uncertainty about whether it would actually help. But from the very first session, I realized that therapy was a safe space where I could be completely honest and vulnerable. It was a place where I didn't have to pretend to be strong, where I could express my fears, my anger, and my sadness without fear of judgment.

My therapist became a guide on my healing journey, helping me to unpack the layers of trauma that I had been carrying for so long. We talked about my mum's death, the immense responsibility I felt as the eldest daughter, and the impact it had on my self-esteem and relationships. Through our sessions, I began to see how deeply these experiences had shaped me—how they had influenced my beliefs about myself, my worth, and what I deserved in life.

One of the most powerful aspects of therapy was the way it helped me to understand my emotions. Before therapy, I often felt like my emotions were out of control, like they were something to be feared or suppressed. But through our work together, I learned that my emotions were not my enemy—they were a natural response to the pain I had experienced. My therapist taught me how to sit with my emotions, to acknowledge them without being overwhelmed by them. This was a game-changer for me. It allowed me to begin the process of healing from the inside out.

Therapy also helped me to recognize patterns in my life that were contributing to my pain. I began to see how my trauma had influenced my relationships, how it had led me to accept less than I deserved, and how it had caused me to put up walls to protect myself from further hurt. With the help of my therapist, I was able to start breaking down those walls, to rebuild my self-esteem, and to create healthier, more fulfilling relationships.

One of the things I appreciated most about therapy was the way it gave me permission to focus on myself. As the eldest daughter, I had spent so much of my life taking care of others that I had forgotten how to take care of myself. Therapy was a reminder that my needs mattered, that my healing was important, and that it was okay to prioritize my well-being. This was a radical shift for me, and it was one that made all the difference.

But therapy wasn't just about talking—it was also about taking action. My therapist encouraged me to try different strategies and techniques to support my healing. We explored mindfulness, meditation, journaling, and other tools that helped me to stay grounded and connected to myself. These practices became a vital part of my healing journey, giving me the strength to keep moving forward even when the road was difficult.

Another critical aspect of therapy was the sense of accountability it provided. Knowing that I had someone who was invested in my healing, who was there to support me every step of the way, made it easier to stay committed to the process. There were times when I wanted to give up, when the pain felt too overwhelming, but having my therapist there to remind me of my progress and to encourage me to keep going was invaluable.

Seeking support through therapy also taught me the importance of community. Healing is not a solitary journey—it's something that we do in connection with others. Whether it's through therapy, support groups, or close friendships, having people in your life who understand what you're going through can make all the difference. These connections provide a sense of belonging, a reminder that you're not alone, and a source of comfort and strength when you need it most.

For anyone considering therapy or counseling, I want to say this: It's okay to ask for help. It's okay to admit that you can't do it all on your own. Seeking support is not a sign of weakness—it's a sign of strength. It takes courage to face your pain, to open up to another person, and to commit to the process of healing. But I can tell you from my own experience that it's worth it. Therapy gave me the tools, the understanding, and the support I needed to heal from my trauma, and it can do the same for you.

If you're unsure about where to start, I encourage you to take that first step. Whether it's reaching out to a therapist, joining a support group, or simply talking to a trusted friend, know that there is help available. Healing is a journey, and you don't have to walk it alone. There are people who want to support you, who have the knowledge and experience to guide you, and who will stand by you as you work through your pain.

As you seek support, remember to be patient with yourself. Healing is not a linear process—it's full of ups and downs, twists and turns. There will be times when you feel like you're making great progress, and other times when it feels like you're stuck or even going backward. This is normal. The important thing is to keep going, to keep seeking support, and to trust that with time and effort, healing is possible.

You are not the first one and definitely not alone. There are so many people out there who have experienced trauma and who are on their own healing journeys. You are part of a larger community of individuals who understand what you're going through, who have faced similar challenges, and who have come out the other side stronger and more resilient. By seeking support, you're not just helping yourself—you're also joining a community of healers, of survivors, and of people who are committed to living their best lives despite the pain they've endured.

There is light at the end of the tunnel, and that with the right support, you will get there. Therapy and counseling are powerful tools that can help you to heal, to grow, and to create the life you deserve. You are worthy of healing, you are worthy of support, and you are worthy of living a life filled with peace, joy, and fulfillment.

Building a support system

Building a support system is one of the most crucial aspects of healing from trauma. It's often said that "no man is an island," and this couldn't be truer when it comes to recovering from deep emotional wounds. When life has knocked you down, having people who can lift you up, walk beside you, and offer their strength when yours falters can make all the difference. In my own journey, finding and leaning on a support system was not just helpful—it was essential.

After losing my mum, I found myself in a position where I had to be strong for my siblings, to take on responsibilities far beyond what a 17-year-old should have to bear. But in those quiet moments when I was alone, I felt utterly overwhelmed, lost, and scared. The weight of grief and responsibility was almost too much to carry on my own. That's when I realized I couldn't do it alone, and that I didn't have to.

My first step in building a support system was acknowledging that I needed help. This wasn't easy. I was so used to being the one people relied on—the one who had it all together, who could handle anything that came her way. Admitting that I was struggling felt like admitting defeat. But the truth is, asking for help isn't a sign of weakness; it's a sign of wisdom and strength. It takes courage to admit that you need others, and it's a crucial step in the healing process.

One of the most important sources of support in my life was my family. Despite the pain we were all going through, we became each other's lifeline. We leaned on one another in ways we hadn't before. In our grief, we found a new kind of closeness, a bond forged in the fires of shared loss. My siblings and I were all hurting, but we also knew that we had to be there for each other. This mutual support became a powerful source of strength.

We didn't have to face our grief alone—we faced it together. We talked about our mum, about the memories we cherished, the things we missed, and the pain we were feeling. It wasn't always easy to talk about these things, but it was necessary. These conversations helped us to process our grief and to understand that it was okay to feel what we were feeling. They also reminded us that we weren't alone in our pain. Having someone who truly understands what you're going through is invaluable, and that's what my siblings were for me.

But family wasn't the only source of support I turned to. I also found strength in my friends and in the community around me. My friends became a safe haven, a place where I could escape the weight of responsibility for a little while. They offered me a shoulder to cry on, an ear to listen, and a heart that cared. They didn't try to fix me or tell me to "move on"; they simply sat with me in my pain, offering their presence and their love.

This kind of support is invaluable. It's not about finding someone who has all the answers or someone who can make the pain go away. It's about finding people who can walk with you through the pain, who can sit with you in the darkness without trying to force the light. Sometimes, all we need is to know that we're not alone—that someone else sees our pain and cares enough to stay with us through it.

In addition to friends and family, I found support in my broader community. Sometimes, this was through formal support groups, where I could connect with others who were also grieving and healing. These groups provided a space where I could share my story, listen to others, and realize that I wasn't alone in my struggles. There's something incredibly healing about being in a room full of people who "get it"—who know what it's like to carry the kind of pain you're carrying. It creates a sense of belonging and shared humanity that can be deeply comforting.

Over time, I also learned that a support system doesn't just have to be made up of people. It can include anything that helps you to feel connected, grounded, and supported. For me, faith played a huge role in my healing process. My relationship with God became a source of strength and comfort during the darkest times. Prayer, meditation, and spiritual practices helped me to find peace, even in the midst of my pain. They reminded me that I was not alone, that there was a higher power guiding me, and that there was hope for healing and renewal.

Creating a support system is about finding what works for you—whether that's friends, family, community, professionals, or your faith. It's about surrounding yourself with people and practices that lift you up, that remind you of your strength, and that help you to keep going when the road gets tough.

One thing I've learned through this journey is that support systems are not static—they change and evolve over time. The people who were there for you at the beginning of your journey might not be the same people who are there as you continue to heal, and that's okay. Healing is a process, and your needs will change as you grow. It's important to be open to these changes and to seek out new sources of support as needed.

If you're in the process of building your own support system, I encourage you to start by looking at the people already in your life. Who can you turn to for support? Who has shown you kindness, compassion, and understanding? Sometimes, we overlook the people who are right in front of us, but they might be the very ones who can offer the support we need.

If you feel like you don't have a strong support system, know that it's never too late to start building one. Reach out to others, whether it's family, friends, or community groups. Don't be afraid to ask for help or to let others know what you're going through. There are people who care, who want to support you, and who will be there for you if you give them the chance.

Building a support system is one of the most important steps you can take on your healing journey. It's about surrounding yourself with love, compassion, and understanding, and about recognizing that you don't have to do it all on your own. Healing is hard work, but it's work that becomes a little easier when you have others by your side. Reach out, connect, and let others help you on this path to healing and wholeness.

The importance of self-compassion

Self-compassion is one of the most transformative tools we can use on our healing journey, yet it's often one of the hardest to practice. In the midst of trauma and grief, we can be our own harshest critics, holding ourselves to impossibly high standards, feeling guilt for things we couldn't control, or blaming ourselves for outcomes that were beyond our influence. I know this all too well from my own experiences, and I want to share with you why self-compassion is so crucial and how it can be a beacon of light in even the darkest moments.

I vividly remember sitting alone in my room, overwhelmed by the sheer magnitude of it all, and feeling a deep sense of guilt. Guilt for not being able to be the perfect caretaker, guilt for not always being present, and guilt for even feeling tired or frustrated. It was as if I was carrying not just the weight of my grief but also the burden of my own expectations and self-criticism.

Trauma and loss are incredibly challenging, and navigating them is no easy feat. It's normal to have moments of doubt, frustration, and even anger. What's crucial is how we respond to these feelings. For me, it took time and reflection to understand that self-compassion was not about ignoring my responsibilities or dismissing my feelings. Instead, it was about recognizing my humanity and treating myself with the same kindness and understanding that I would offer a loved one in a similar situation.

Self-compassion is about acknowledging that we are doing our best in difficult circumstances and giving ourselves permission to be imperfect. It means understanding that it's okay to feel overwhelmed, to make mistakes, and to have moments where we fall short of our own expectations. When I began to practice self-compassion, I started to shift from a place of self-criticism to one of understanding and acceptance.

One of the most powerful ways I learned to practice self-compassion was by challenging my inner critic. I started to ask myself, "Would I speak to a friend this way?" The answer was always no. I wouldn't berate a friend for their struggles or for not being perfect; I would offer them support, empathy, and encouragement. This realization helped me to extend the same kindness to myself.

Another key aspect of self-compassion is recognizing that it's okay to prioritize self-care. During the early days of my grief, I felt that taking time for myself was a luxury I couldn't afford. But the truth is, self-care is essential for healing. It's not selfish; it's necessary. Taking time to rest, to engage in activities that bring joy, and to nurture ourselves is crucial for our well-being and our ability to cope with the demands of trauma.

It's also important to remember that self-compassion involves embracing our imperfections. We are all human, and we all have limitations. Accepting this can relieve some of the pressure we put on ourselves. For me, this meant acknowledging that I couldn't always be the perfect sibling or the perfect person. I could only do my best with the resources and energy I had at the time. And that was enough.

In my own journey, I also found that connecting with others who had experienced similar struggles was incredibly helpful. Sharing my story with people who understood my pain allowed me to feel seen and validated. It was through these connections that I learned that my feelings were normal and that I wasn't alone in my struggles. This sense of shared experience helped me to be kinder to myself and to recognize that I was not isolated in my suffering.

Self-compassion also involves forgiving ourselves. It's easy to hold onto regrets and to replay moments of perceived failure in our minds. But holding onto these regrets only prolongs our suffering. Forgiveness is a powerful act of self-compassion. It means letting go of the burden of self-blame and accepting that we did the best we could in the given circumstances.

Practicing self-compassion is an ongoing process. There are days when it's easier to be kind to ourselves and days when it feels more challenging. What's important is to continue to nurture this practice, to remind ourselves that we are worthy of kindness, and to offer ourselves the same support and love that we would give to others.

If you're struggling with self-compassion, I encourage you to start small. Begin by acknowledging your feelings without judgment. When you notice self-critical thoughts, gently challenge them and replace them with more compassionate ones. Remember that healing is a journey, and it's okay to take it one step at a time.

One powerful practice is to keep a self-compassion journal. Write down moments when you've been hard on yourself and then rewrite those moments with a more compassionate perspective. Reflect on the things you've done well, the times you've shown strength, and the ways you've cared for yourself and others. This exercise can help shift your mindset from self-criticism to self-acceptance.

Another practice is to use affirmations. Simple statements like "I am doing my best" or "I am worthy of love and care" can serve as reminders to treat yourself with kindness. These affirmations can be especially helpful during moments of self-doubt or guilt.

Many of us struggle with self-compassion, and it's okay to seek support in developing this practice. Surround yourself with people who uplift and encourage you, and don't hesitate to reach out for help if you need it.

Self-compassion is not about denying the challenges or difficulties we face; it's about approaching ourselves with understanding and kindness in the midst of those challenges. It's about recognizing that we are all doing the best we can and that we deserve compassion and care, both from others and from ourselves.

I hope you find ways to embrace self-compassion and to be gentle with yourself. Healing takes time, and it's a process filled with ups and downs. Through it all, remember that you are deserving of kindness, that you are not alone, and that you have the strength to navigate your path to healing with compassion and grace.

Reclaiming Your Power

Reclaiming your power after trauma is a profound and personal journey. It's about taking back control of your life and your well-being when everything around you feels as if it's spiraling out of control. For me, this journey began with a simple yet transformative realization: I had the ability to shape my path forward, despite the overwhelming odds.

The first step to reclaiming my power was acknowledging that it was okay to feel vulnerable. For a long time, I resisted accepting my own vulnerability. I thought that admitting how much I was struggling meant I was weak or incapable. But the truth is, vulnerability is a part of being human, and accepting it was a crucial step in taking back control.

I began to see vulnerability not as a sign of weakness but as a gateway to personal growth and empowerment. By allowing myself to fully experience and process my emotions, I was able to gain clarity about what I truly needed to heal and move forward. This acceptance of vulnerability was liberating—it allowed me to stop fighting against my own feelings and to start addressing them with compassion and understanding.

Next, I focused on setting boundaries. In the wake of my mum's death, I was constantly being pulled in different directions. Everyone had their expectations, and it felt like I was juggling a million things at once. But I realized that to reclaim my power, I needed to set clear boundaries for myself. This meant saying no when I needed to, prioritizing my own well-being, and making space for self-care.

Setting boundaries was not easy. It meant confronting the fear of disappointing others and dealing with the guilt that came with it. But it was essential for my own healing. I started by identifying what was truly important to me and what I could realistically handle. I learned to communicate my needs and limitations clearly, and I practiced honoring those boundaries with kindness and respect.

Another significant aspect of reclaiming my power was taking control of my narrative. For a long time, I felt defined by my grief and the role I had been thrust into. It was as if my identity had been reduced to my loss and my responsibilities. But I began to realize that I had the power to shape my own story, to define who I was beyond my trauma.

I started to focus on the things that brought me joy and fulfillment. I made a conscious effort to pursue activities that aligned with my passions and values. This was not about escaping my grief but about integrating it into a new and empowered sense of self. By rediscovering and nurturing my interests, I began to rebuild my sense of identity and purpose.

Reclaiming my power also involved building resilience. Trauma can leave us feeling fragile and vulnerable, but resilience is about developing the inner strength to bounce back from adversity. It's about finding ways to adapt and thrive despite the challenges we face.

I built resilience by focusing on my strengths and celebrating my progress, no matter how small. I learned to view setbacks as opportunities for growth rather than as failures. I surrounded myself with supportive people who encouraged me and believed in my ability to overcome obstacles. And I practiced self-compassion, recognizing that resilience is a journey, not a destination.

Another key aspect of reclaiming power was setting goals and taking action. When we're dealing with trauma, it's easy to feel stuck or overwhelmed. Setting small, achievable goals gave me a sense of direction and purpose. It allowed me to take concrete steps towards creating a life that felt meaningful and fulfilling.

These goals didn't have to be grand or ambitious. They could be as simple as making time for a daily walk, reaching out to a friend for support, or dedicating time to a creative project. The important thing was to set goals that were aligned with my values and that contributed to my healing process.

As I worked towards these goals, I celebrated my successes and acknowledged my efforts. This practice helped me to build confidence and to reinforce the belief that I had the power to shape my own path. It also reminded me that progress is not always linear and that every step forward, no matter how small, is a victory.

Reclaiming your power is a deeply personal journey, and it's important to honor your own process. It's okay to take things one step at a time and to be gentle with yourself as you navigate this path. Remember that reclaiming power is not about controlling every aspect of your life but about finding the strength to make choices that support your well-being and growth.

To reclaim your power? I encourage you to embrace the process with patience and compassion. Recognize that healing takes time and that it's normal to have ups and downs along the way. Trust in your own strength and resilience, and know that you have the power to create a life that feels meaningful and fulfilling. You have the ability to reclaim your power, to take control of your healing journey, and to build a life that reflects your true self.

Healing Through Self-Reflection

Self-reflection is a powerful tool in the journey of healing from trauma. It offers a space for introspection, allowing us to process our experiences, understand our emotions, and gain clarity about our path forward. Self-reflection, particularly through journaling, must become a crucial part of your healing process. It is more than just putting pen to paper; it's about connecting with yourself in a deep and meaningful way.

Journaling, in its simplest form, is the act of writing down your thoughts and feelings. But its benefits go far beyond that. When we write, we create a tangible space to explore our inner world. It allows us to externalize our thoughts and feelings, making them easier to confront and understand. This act of putting thoughts into words can be incredibly therapeutic.

For me, journaling started as a way to vent my frustrations and sort through my emotions. I would write about the things that were troubling me, the challenges I was facing, and the memories that haunted me. At first, it was just an outlet, a way to get everything out of my head and onto paper. But as I continued to journal, I began to notice patterns and insights that I hadn't seen before.

One of the most profound realizations I had through journaling was the way my trauma was affecting my daily life. As I wrote about my interactions with others, my reactions to stress, and my general outlook on life, I started to see how my unresolved grief was influencing my behavior and relationships. It was like holding up a mirror to my soul and seeing the impact of my trauma reflected back at me.

Journaling also provided a space for me to explore my feelings of guilt and self-blame. After my mum's death, I often felt that I wasn't doing enough or that I was failing in my role as a caregiver. Through writing, I could examine these feelings more closely. I would ask myself why I felt this way and where these feelings were coming from. This process of questioning and exploring helped me to confront and eventually release some of the guilt that had been weighing me down.

Another important aspect of self-reflection through journaling was the ability to track my progress. Healing is not a linear process; it comes with its ups and downs. Journaling allowed me to see how far I had come, even when it didn't feel like it. I could look back at my earlier entries and see the growth and changes that had occurred over time. This perspective was incredibly validating and motivating.

Self-reflection through journaling also gave me a way to set intentions and goals for my healing journey. By writing about what I wanted to achieve, I could clarify my priorities and create actionable steps. This practice helped me to stay focused and to navigate my healing process with purpose. It also provided a way to celebrate my achievements, no matter how small, and to acknowledge the efforts I was making towards my recovery.

In addition to journaling, self-reflection can also involve other practices such as meditation, mindfulness, or engaging in creative activities. These practices can complement the insights gained through writing and provide additional ways to connect with yourself. For me, combining journaling with moments of stillness and reflection created a more holistic approach to my healing process.

It's important to remember that self-reflection is a personal journey, and there is no right or wrong way to do it. What works for one person may not work for another, and that's okay. The key is to find a practice that resonates with you and to make it a regular part of your healing process. Whether it's through journaling, meditation, or another form of self-expression, the goal is to create a space for yourself to explore and understand your inner world.

I encourage you to approach it with openness and curiosity. Allow yourself to explore your thoughts and feelings without judgment. Be patient with yourself and recognize that self-reflection is an ongoing process. It's about creating a dialogue with yourself and discovering the wisdom and strength that lies within.

Remember that healing is not about achieving perfection but about finding peace and understanding within yourself. Self-reflection can be a powerful tool in this process, helping you to navigate your emotions, set intentions, and build a deeper connection with yourself. Embrace this journey with compassion and patience, and know that you are worthy of the healing and growth that comes from within.

Embracing Forgiveness

Forgiveness is often seen as a gift we give to others, but one of the most profound acts of forgiveness we can offer is to ourselves. This chapter is about embracing forgiveness, especially the act of forgiving ourselves for not being perfect during difficult times. It's about recognizing that our struggles and imperfections are part of our journey and learning to extend the same grace and compassion to ourselves that we would offer to others.

When we are in the midst of trauma or pain, it's easy to fall into the trap of self-blame and harsh self-criticism. We think we should be handling things better, that we should be stronger, or that we should be able to "fix" everything immediately. I remember feeling this way myself. I put immense pressure on myself to be perfect—to somehow be strong, to manage everything, and to stay composed despite the whirlwind of emotions I was experiencing.

The truth is, none of us are perfect, especially when we're facing the kinds of challenges that come with trauma. It's okay to stumble, to falter, and to feel like you're not measuring up. In fact, it's more than okay—it's human. Recognizing this and allowing ourselves to be imperfect is a crucial step in the process of self-forgiveness.

Forgiving yourself doesn't mean excusing mistakes or overlooking areas where you might have fallen short. Instead, it means acknowledging that you did the best you could with what you had at the time. It's about understanding that while you may have made mistakes or faced limitations, those experiences do not define your worth or your future.

One of the first steps in embracing self-forgiveness is to confront the guilt and self-blame that often accompany difficult times. Guilt can be particularly harsh when you're trying to navigate through trauma. You might feel guilty for not being able to provide more support, for not being strong enough, or for not reacting the way you think you should have. I certainly felt this way, especially when I looked back on my actions and choices during those early days of grief and responsibility.

However, it's important to recognize that guilt, while a natural emotion, is not always a helpful one. It can keep us trapped in a cycle of self-criticism and prevent us from moving forward. Forgiveness begins with challenging these feelings of guilt and understanding that they are a part of the healing process but not a reflection of our entire experience or identity.

Start by acknowledging your feelings of guilt or regret. Write them down if that helps. Then, take a step back and ask yourself if you would judge someone else as harshly as you judge yourself. More often than not, we are our own worst critics. When we hold ourselves to impossibly high standards, we forget that we're human, with limitations and vulnerabilities.

Forgiveness also involves letting go of the need to be perfect. It's about accepting that making mistakes is a part of being human and that our worth isn't tied to our ability to be flawless. For me, this realization was liberating. I learned that it was okay to not have all the answers, to not always be strong, and to ask for help when I needed it. It was a crucial lesson in understanding that my value wasn't contingent on my ability to handle everything on my own.

Self-forgiveness is understanding that healing is a journey, not a destination. It's okay to have setbacks and moments of struggle along the way. The process of forgiveness is ongoing, and it requires patience and compassion. Be gentle with yourself as you navigate this journey. Recognize that self-forgiveness isn't about erasing the past or forgetting the pain— it's about making peace with it and moving forward with a sense of understanding and acceptance.

One practical way to embrace forgiveness is through positive self-talk. Instead of focusing on what you think you did wrong, shift your attention to the ways in which you've shown strength and resilience. Remind yourself of the times you've overcome challenges and the progress you've made. Positive self talk can help to reframe your thoughts and reinforce a kinder, more compassionate perspective toward yourself.

Forgiving yourself is an essential part of finding peace after pain. It allows you to release the burden of self-blame and to embrace your humanity. It's about understanding that you did the best you could in the circumstances you were given and recognizing that your worth is not defined by your mistakes or imperfections. By practicing self-forgiveness, you pave the way for healing, growth, and a renewed sense of self-compassion.

Forgiving Others: Letting Go of Resentment

This aspect of forgiveness was challenging yet essential in my journey towards healing. It involved confronting and releasing feelings of resentment and disappointment, particularly towards those who were absent or unsupportive during one of the most difficult times in my life.

I felt angry at people who I believed should have been there for me but weren't. There were friends who drifted away, family members who seemed to avoid the discomfort of my grief, and a world that continued to spin despite my personal tragedy. I felt let down and isolated, and these feelings of resentment began to weigh heavily on me.

Resentment is a natural response when we feel unsupported or abandoned. It's our mind's way of processing the hurt and injustice we've experienced. However, holding onto this resentment can become a major obstacle in our healing journey. It keeps us tied to the pain and prevents us from moving forward.

One of the first steps in working through resentment is to acknowledge and accept your feelings. I had to come to terms with the fact that it was okay to feel angry and upset about the lack of support I received. This acceptance was the first step towards letting go.

Next, I began to explore the reasons behind the absence of support. Often, people who don't provide the support we need are not necessarily acting out of malice. They may be dealing with their own struggles, or they might simply not know how to offer the help we need. Understanding this can help shift our perspective and reduce the intensity of our resentment. It's not about excusing their behavior but about recognizing that their actions are more about their limitations than a reflection of our worth.

In my case, I came to understand that many people in my life were simply overwhelmed by their own circumstances. They might have wanted to help but didn't know how or felt incapable of providing the support I needed. This realization didn't erase the hurt, but it did help me see their actions in a different light. It allowed me to move from a place of anger to a place of compassion and understanding.

Another crucial step in forgiving others is to communicate your feelings, if possible and appropriate. For some, having an honest conversation with those who were absent or unsupportive can provide closure and help mend relationships. However, this step may not always be feasible or beneficial for everyone. In my own journey, I found that expressing my feelings through writing or therapy was a valuable alternative when direct communication wasn't possible.

Forgiveness doesn't mean you have to forget or continue to invest in relationships that were harmful or unsupportive. It's about releasing the hold that resentment has on you, so you can move forward with a lighter heart. It's a way of freeing yourself from the burden of carrying anger and disappointment.

One technique that helped me in this process was writing forgiveness letters. These letters were not always intended to be sent; rather, they served as a way for me to articulate my feelings and release them. I wrote letters to people who I felt had let me down, expressing my hurt and my decision to let go of the resentment. This practice was cathartic and empowering, allowing me to take control of my emotions and begin the process of healing.

Forgiveness is also about redefining your relationship with the past. It's about choosing to let go of the power that past hurts have over your present and future. For me, this meant actively working to shift my focus from the pain of what was lacking to the gratitude for what I had and the progress I was making. It's about recognizing that while the support I needed wasn't always there, I was still capable of finding strength and resilience within myself.

As you embark on your own journey of forgiveness, remember that it's a process that takes time. Be patient with yourself and recognize that it's okay to have mixed emotions along the way. Forgiving others doesn't mean you're condoning their actions; it means you're choosing to let go of the hold those actions have on you.

Ultimately, embracing forgiveness is about finding peace within yourself. It's about releasing the burden of resentment and allowing yourself to move forward with a lighter heart. Through forgiveness, you can create space for healing, growth, and a renewed sense of self-compassion.

Remember that forgiveness is a gift you give to yourself. It's about liberating yourself from the pain of the past and stepping into a future where you can live with greater freedom and peace.

Rebuilding Your Life

Rebuilding your life after experiencing profound trauma is very hard. The damage can be overwhelming, and starting over often feels daunting. I however learned that rebuilding isn't just about fixing what was broken; it's about creating something new and meaningful from the pieces left behind. I'm sharing the steps I took to rebuild my life and how you can approach your own journey with resilience and hope.

Accepting the New Reality

The first step in rebuilding my life was accepting the new reality. Grief and trauma often leave us clinging to the past, yearning for what once was. Accepting that things would never be the same was a painful but necessary part of my journey. It was about coming to terms with the fact that my mum was gone, and I had to find a way to move forward.

This acceptance didn't come overnight. It required me to face my emotions head-on and acknowledge the depth of my loss. I had to let go of the fantasy that I could somehow return to the way things were before. Instead, I began to accept that my life had fundamentally changed, and I needed to find a new way to live it.

Accepting my new reality involved setting aside time to grieve and process my emotions. I allowed myself to feel sadness, anger, and confusion without judgment. Through this process, I began to understand that acceptance was not about forgetting or moving on quickly but about embracing the reality of my situation and finding a way to rebuild from there.

Setting Small, Achievable Goals

Once I accepted my new reality, the next step was setting small, achievable goals. Rebuilding my life felt like an enormous task, so breaking it down into manageable steps helped me to make progress without feeling overwhelmed.

I started with simple goals: creating a daily routine, managing household responsibilities, and taking care of myself physically and emotionally. Each small goal was a victory, a step towards regaining control over my life. As I achieved these smaller goals, I gained confidence and a sense of accomplishment that motivated me to tackle more significant challenges.

For instance, setting a goal to establish a consistent sleep schedule helped me to improve my overall well-being. Planning and preparing meals for my siblings was another small goal that gave me a sense of purpose and stability. Each achievement, no matter how small, contributed to the larger process of rebuilding my life.

Rediscovering Your Passions

As I rebuilt my life, rediscovering my passions was an essential part of the process. Trauma and grief can overshadow our interests and passions, making it difficult to find joy in the things we once loved. Reconnecting with activities that brought me joy and fulfillment helped me to find purpose and meaning in my new reality.

I took up hobbies that I had once enjoyed, such as writing, painting, and spending time in nature. Engaging in these activities provided me with a sense of normalcy and allowed me to express my emotions in a creative way. Rediscovering my passions helped me to rebuild my sense of self and find joy amidst the pain.

If you're struggling to find joy after trauma, consider exploring activities that you once loved or trying something new. Rediscovering your passions can help you to reconnect with yourself and find fulfillment in your journey of healing.

Creating New Traditions

Part of rebuilding my life involved creating new traditions and routines. The traditions I had with my mum were precious, but I realized that I needed to create new ones that reflected my current reality and supported my healing process.

I started by establishing new family rituals, such as weekly game nights, cooking meals together, and celebrating small victories. These new traditions provided a sense of continuity and stability in my life. They also helped me to create positive memories and foster a sense of connection with my siblings.

Creating new traditions can be a powerful way to honor your journey and build a new sense of normalcy. It's about finding ways to incorporate joy and meaning into your daily life, even amidst the challenges.

Embracing Personal Growth

Rebuilding my life also involved embracing personal growth. Trauma and grief can be transformative experiences that offer opportunities for growth and self-discovery. As I worked through my emotions and challenges, I began to recognize the strengths and resilience I had developed.

Personal growth involved reflecting on my experiences, learning from them, and using them to shape a new perspective on life. I explored new areas of interest, pursued personal development opportunities, and embraced a mindset of growth and learning.

If you're rebuilding your life, consider how you can use your experiences as opportunities for growth. Reflect on what you've learned, how you've changed, and how you can continue to grow and evolve.

Finding Meaning and Purpose

Finding meaning and purpose in the aftermath of trauma was a critical aspect of rebuilding my life. I had to search for ways to make sense of my experiences and find purpose in my new reality. This search for meaning helped me to create a sense of direction and motivation.

I explored ways to use my experiences to help others, such as volunteering, sharing my story, and supporting others who were going through similar challenges. Finding meaning in my journey gave me a renewed sense of purpose and allowed me to make a positive impact in the lives of others.

Finding meaning and purpose can be a powerful way to rebuild your life. Consider how you can use your experiences to contribute to the well-being of others and create a sense of purpose in your journey.

Rebuilding my life was a journey, not a destination. It involved continuous effort, reflection, and growth. Embracing the journey meant accepting that there would be ups and downs, and that healing is a process that takes time.

As you rebuild your life, remember that it's a journey that unfolds over time. Embrace each step of the process, celebrate your progress, and remain hopeful for the future.

Through my own experience, I learned that rebuilding is not just about fixing what was broken but about creating something new and meaningful. It's about finding hope amidst the pain and building a life that reflects your resilience and strength.

How I set new goals and created a vision for my future.

I discovered that setting new goals and creating a vision for my future were crucial steps in finding my way. I share how I approached this process, and how you can, too, with hope and determination.

Finding Clarity in Chaos

The first step in setting new goals and creating a vision was finding clarity amid the chaos. After the initial shock and pain of losing my mum, I needed to understand what I wanted for my future. This required taking a step back from the immediate struggles and reflecting on what truly mattered to me.

I began by asking myself a series of questions: What are my core values? What brings me joy? What kind of future do I envision for myself? These questions were not easy to answer, especially amidst the haze of grief, but they were essential in guiding me toward a clearer sense of direction.

Finding clarity involved spending time in quiet reflection, journaling, and having honest conversations with myself about my desires and goals. It was a process of sorting through the noise and focusing on what was most important to me. It's important to allow yourself this space to reflect, as it can lead to a deeper understanding of your aspirations and priorities.

Once I had some clarity, the next step was setting small, achievable goals.This meant being realistic about what I could handle at any given time. It meant acknowledging my limits and not setting myself up for failure. These small, incremental steps were crucial in creating a foundation upon which I could build more ambitious goals.

Creating a Vision Board

To help visualize my future, I created a vision board. This was a tangible representation of my goals, dreams, and aspirations. I gathered images, quotes, and symbols that represented what I wanted to achieve and placed them on a board where I could see them daily.

Creating a vision board was a powerful way to keep my goals front and center. It served as a daily reminder of what I was working toward and provided motivation when I felt discouraged. It also helped me to focus on the positive aspects of my future rather than being consumed by past pain.

If you're feeling lost or uncertain about your future, consider creating a vision board. It can be a creative and effective way to clarify your goals and keep them in view as you work toward rebuilding your life.

Embracing Flexibility

As I set new goals and created a vision for my future, I learned the importance of embracing flexibility. Life after trauma is unpredictable, and my plans needed to be adaptable to changing circumstances. This flexibility allowed me to adjust my goals as needed and respond to new challenges with resilience.

Embracing flexibility meant recognizing that it was okay for my goals to evolve over time. I learned to let go of rigid expectations and instead focus on staying open to new opportunities and directions. This approach helped me to navigate the uncertainties of my journey with greater ease and adaptability. Be willing to adjust your goals and vision as needed, and trust that flexibility can lead to new and unexpected opportunities.

Celebrating Milestones

As I made progress toward my goals, celebrating milestones became an important part of the process. Each achievement, no matter how small, was a testament to my resilience and effort. Celebrating these milestones provided a sense of accomplishment and reinforced my commitment to my goals.

Celebrating milestones involved acknowledging my progress and taking time to reflect on how far I had come. It also meant recognizing and appreciating the small victories along the way. Celebrating these moments helped to maintain a positive outlook and motivated me to continue working toward my vision.

Staying Committed to Your Vision

Rebuilding your life is a long-term process that requires commitment. Staying focused on your vision and goals, even when faced with setbacks, is essential in achieving the future you envision. This commitment involved maintaining a positive attitude, persevering through challenges, and continuously working toward my goals.

Staying committed to my vision meant regularly reviewing and adjusting my goals as needed. It also involved setting aside time to reflect on my progress and make any necessary changes. By staying dedicated to my vision, I was able to navigate obstacles and continue moving forward.

Rebuilding your life is a journey that unfolds over time. It involves continuous effort, reflection, and growth. Embracing this journey means accepting that there will be ups and downs, and that healing is a process that takes time.

Throughout this journey, it's important to celebrate your progress, no matter how small. Embrace each step of the process with hope and perseverance, and trust that you have the strength to create a new and fulfilling life.

Cultivating Resilience

Techniques for Maintaining Peace During Tough Times

When the weight of grief and trauma presses down on you, finding a path to peace can seem daunting. For me, the most profound source of comfort and resilience came from my faith—through prayer, the Bible, and my relationship with God. These spiritual practices became my lifelines, guiding me through the darkest times and helping me reclaim a sense of peace. If you're navigating similar struggles, let me share how leaning into God and the scriptures can provide solace and strength.

Anchoring in Prayer

Prayer became my anchor during the tumultuous times of my grief. It was in those quiet moments of conversation with God that I found a reprieve from the overwhelming pain. Prayer allowed me to express my deepest fears, sorrows, and hopes. I remember sitting in my room, the silence around me only broken by the whispered words of my prayers. It was there, in that sacred space, that I felt God's presence most intensely.

In Philippians 4:6-7, the Bible assures us: "Do not be anxious about anything, but in every situation, by prayer and petition, with thanksgiving, present your requests to God. And the peace of God, which transcends all understanding, will guard your hearts and your minds in Christ Jesus." This passage was a beacon of hope for me. It reminded me that, through prayer, I could bring my burdens before God and trust that His peace would envelop me.

I made it a daily practice to pray, even when the words were hard to find. Sometimes, my prayers were simple pleas for strength or comfort. Other times, they were expressions of gratitude for the little moments of peace I found amidst the chaos. Regardless of the form they took, these conversations with God were a source of profound comfort and guidance.

Finding Solace in Scripture

The Bible became my guide and source of comfort as I navigated through my grief. Scriptures provided me with reassurance and wisdom, offering a sense of stability in the midst of emotional turbulence. When my mum passed away, I turned to passages that spoke to the heartache and the hope of renewal.

Psalm 34:18 was particularly meaningful: "The Lord is close to the brokenhearted and saves those who are crushed in spirit." Reading this verse reminded me that, even in my deepest sorrow, God was near. The Bible's promises became a balm for my wounded soul, assuring me of God's steadfast love and presence.

I found great comfort in passages that spoke of God's plans for us, such as Jeremiah 29:11: "For I know the plans I have for you, declares the Lord, plans to prosper you and not to harm you, plans to give you hope and a future." These verses helped me to see beyond my immediate pain and trust in God's broader plan for my life.

In times of distress, I would open my Bible and read passages that resonated with my situation. Sometimes, it was a specific verse that seemed to speak directly to my heart. Other times, it was the overall message of hope and perseverance that provided comfort. Engaging with scripture in this way helped me to maintain a sense of connection with God and reinforced my faith that I was not alone in my journey.

Embracing God's Promises

Embracing the promises of God was crucial in maintaining peace during my healing process. The Bible is filled with assurances of God's love, care, and faithfulness. These promises provided a foundation upon which I could build my resilience.

One promise that stood out to me was found in Isaiah 41:10: "So do not fear, for I am with you; do not be dismayed, for I am your God. I will strengthen you and help you; I will uphold you with my righteous right hand." This verse was a powerful reminder that, even when I felt alone and overwhelmed, God's strength was available to me. It helped me confront my fears and embrace the healing process with a sense of divine support.

Another promise that gave me comfort was Romans 8:28: "And we know that in all things God works for the good of those who love him, who have been called according to his purpose." This verse reassured me that, despite the pain and challenges, God was working for my good. It helped me trust that there was a purpose behind my suffering and that healing and growth were possible.

Finding Peace in God's Presence

Experiencing God's presence was a central part of my journey to peace. During my most difficult moments, I would often seek solitude, finding comfort in the quiet and allowing myself to be fully present with God. In these moments, I felt an overwhelming sense of calm and reassurance.

Psalm 46:10 invites us to "Be still, and know that I am God." Practicing stillness and seeking God's presence helped me to quiet my anxious thoughts and embrace a deeper sense of peace. By setting aside time for meditation and reflection, I was able to connect with God in a meaningful way, finding solace in His presence.

In my daily routine, I incorporated practices that facilitated this connection, such as reading devotionals, listening to uplifting worship music, and spending time in nature. These activities helped me to stay focused on God and His promises, reinforcing my sense of peace and stability.

Trusting in God's Plan

Trusting in God's plan for my life was a significant aspect of maintaining peace during my healing journey. The Bible reassures us that God has a purpose for each of us, even when we can't see it clearly.

Proverbs 3:5-6 encourages us to "Trust in the Lord with all your heart and lean not on your own understanding; in all your ways submit to him, and he will make your paths straight."

Trusting in God's plan required me to let go of my own need to control every aspect of my life and to have faith that He was guiding me toward a greater purpose.

When I faced setbacks or struggled with uncertainty, I reminded myself of God's sovereignty and His ability to bring good out of even the most challenging situations. This trust provided me with a sense of hope and direction, helping me to maintain peace and resilience in the face of adversity.

Maintaining peace during tough times is a journey that involves leaning into our faith, embracing God's promises, and finding solace in prayer and scripture. Through my own experiences, I have learned that God's presence, promises, and support are powerful sources of comfort and resilience. By anchoring ourselves in these spiritual practices, we can navigate the challenges of life with a sense of peace and hope. If you find yourself struggling, I encourage you to seek God's presence, immerse yourself in His word, and trust in His plan for your life. In doing so, you may find the strength and peace you need to overcome the obstacles you face.

Finding Joy Again

The journey to finding joy again involves embracing the present moment and fully living in the here and now. In this chapter I'm exploring how we can reconnect with joy, focusing on practical strategies and insights from personal experience.

Embracing the Present Moment

The concept of living fully in the present moment might sound simple, but it often requires a shift in perspective and intentional effort. After trauma, our minds can become preoccupied with past pain or future anxieties, making it difficult to appreciate the present. However, by grounding ourselves in the here and now, we can begin to experience joy again.

One effective way to embrace the present moment is through mindfulness. Mindfulness involves paying full attention to the current moment without judgment. Whether you're enjoying a meal, spending time with loved ones, or taking a quiet moment alone, try to be fully engaged. Notice the sights, sounds, smells, and sensations of the moment. This practice helps you connect with the present and find joy in the everyday experiences of life.

Living Fully in the Here and Now

Living fully in the present involves more than just being mindful; it's about actively engaging with life and appreciating the beauty of the ordinary. When we focus on today, we give ourselves the opportunity to experience the joy that each moment can offer.

One way to practice this is by setting aside time each day to engage in activities that bring you happiness and fulfillment. This could be anything from a hobby you enjoy, spending time with friends or family, or simply taking a moment to appreciate nature. By making time for activities that nourish your soul, you invite joy into your life.

Cultivating a Heart of Gratitude

Gratitude is a powerful tool for reconnecting with joy. When we focus on what we are thankful for, we shift our perspective away from what we've lost or what we lack. Gratitude helps us recognize the positive aspects of our current situation and find joy in them.

Consider starting a gratitude journal where you write down things you are grateful for each day. This practice can help you develop a habit of recognizing and appreciating the good things in your life. Even on tough days, finding something to be thankful for can shift your focus and help you experience moments of joy.

Finding Joy in Everyday Activities

Joy can often be found in the simplest of everyday activities. By approaching daily routines with a sense of appreciation and mindfulness, you can discover joy in the ordinary. Whether it's savoring a cup of coffee, enjoying a walk in the park, or spending quality time with loved ones, these moments can bring happiness when you fully engage with them.

Think about the activities that bring you joy and make them a regular part of your life. This could be something as simple as reading a book, listening to your favorite music, or cooking a meal. By incorporating these joyful activities into your routine, you create opportunities for happiness and fulfillment.

Creating Joyful Rituals

Incorporating joyful rituals into your daily routine can help you embrace the present and find joy in your life. Rituals are regular practices or routines that bring a sense of comfort and happiness. They can be simple and personal, such as a morning routine that includes a moment of reflection, or a weekly tradition with friends or family.

Creating and maintaining these rituals helps you celebrate the present moment and appreciate the small joys in life. For example, you might start each day with a moment of gratitude, or end your week with a relaxing activity that brings you joy. These rituals provide stability and create opportunities for joy in your daily life.

Engaging with Nature

Spending time in nature can be a powerful way to reconnect with joy and embrace the present. Nature has a way of grounding us and reminding us of the beauty and wonder of the world. Whether it's a walk in the park, a hike in the mountains, or simply sitting outside and observing the natural world, nature can provide a sense of peace and joy.

Take time to appreciate the beauty of the world around you. Notice the colors of the sky, the sounds of birds, and the feeling of the breeze. Engaging with nature can help you feel more connected to the present moment and find joy in the simple pleasures of life.

Using Positive Affirmations

Positive affirmations can be a helpful tool for cultivating joy and focusing on the present. By repeating encouraging and uplifting statements, you can shift your mindset and reinforce a positive outlook. Positive affirmations help you focus on what's good in your life and encourage a sense of optimism and joy.

Create a list of positive affirmations that resonate with you and repeat them daily. These could be statements like, "I am grateful for today," or "I choose to embrace joy in the present moment." Using affirmations can help you maintain a positive mindset and open yourself up to experiencing joy.

Focusing on New Beginnings

Focusing on new beginnings can help you embrace joy and move forward from past pain. Life is full of opportunities for renewal and growth. By setting new goals and embracing new experiences, you create a sense of hope and excitement for the future.

Think about the new beginnings you would like to pursue and take steps towards them. Whether it's starting a new hobby, setting personal goals, or exploring new opportunities, embracing new beginnings can help you find joy and create a positive outlook on life.

Finding joy again after loss or trauma is a journey that involves embracing the present moment, cultivating gratitude, and engaging in joyful activities. By practicing mindfulness, creating joyful rituals, spending time in nature, using positive affirmations, and focusing on new beginnings, you can reconnect with a sense of joy and fulfillment.

Joy is not about eliminating all pain but about finding light and hope even amidst challenges. By making these practices a part of your life, you can embrace the present and live fully, discovering moments of joy and happiness along the way.

Conclusion

Reflecting on the Journey Towards Healing

As we come to the end of this book, I want to take a moment to reflect with you on the journey we've traveled together. Healing from trauma is not a destination but a journey—one that's often long, winding, and filled with ups and downs. But it's also a journey filled with hope, growth, and the promise of a brighter future.

When I look back on my own experiences, I see how far I've come. There were days when I thought the pain would never end, when the weight of my grief felt unbearable. But there were also moments of light—moments when I felt God's presence so clearly, guiding me, comforting me, and reminding me that I wasn't alone. I've shared my story with you in the hopes that it might help you feel less alone in your own journey, that it might offer you some comfort and inspiration as you navigate your path to healing.

Reflecting on Your Journey

Now, I want to encourage you to take some time to reflect on your own journey. Think about where you started, where you are now, and the progress you've made along the way. Healing from trauma is not linear—it's not a straight line from pain to peace. There are setbacks, challenges, and moments when it feels like you're back at square one. But every step you've taken, no matter how small, is a step towards healing.

Take a moment to acknowledge your strength and resilience. You've made it this far, and that's something to be proud of. You've faced your pain head-on, you've sought out support, and you've taken steps to heal. That takes courage—more courage than most people realize. So, give yourself some grace, and recognize the progress you've made, even if it doesn't always feel like progress.

Continuing the Healing Process

As I've said before, healing is an ongoing process. It doesn't end when you close this book or when you've reached a certain milestone. It's a lifelong journey, and that's okay. The important thing is that you keep moving forward, even when it's hard. Keep seeking out the support you need, keep turning to God for strength and guidance, and keep working on the things that bring you peace and joy.

In my own life, I've found that healing doesn't mean forgetting or erasing the past. Instead, it means finding a way to live with the past, to integrate it into who I am, and to use it as a source of strength and compassion. The pain I've experienced has shaped me, but it doesn't define me. And the same is true for you. Your trauma is a part of your story, but it's not the whole story. There is so much more to you than the pain you've endured.

One of the most important things I've learned on my healing journey is the importance of turning to God. The Bible tells us in Psalm 34:18 that "The Lord is close to the brokenhearted and saves those who are crushed in spirit." This verse has been a source of comfort for me during some of my darkest moments. Knowing that God is close to me, even when I'm hurting, has given me the strength to keep going. And I hope it can do the same for you.

Leaning on God in the Healing Process

The Bible is full of stories of people who faced incredible pain and hardship, but who found strength and hope in God. One of my favorite stories is that of Joseph in the Old Testament. Joseph was betrayed by his brothers, sold into slavery, and endured years of suffering. But through it all, he remained faithful to God, and in the end, God used his pain for a greater purpose. In Genesis 50:20, Joseph says to his brothers, "You intended to harm me, but God intended it for good to accomplish what is now being done, the saving of many lives."

This story is a powerful reminder that God can use even our deepest pain for good. It doesn't mean that the pain isn't real or that it doesn't matter—it does. But it means that God can take our pain and turn it into something beautiful, something that can help others and bring glory to Him.

As you continue on your healing journey, I encourage you to lean on God. Turn to Him in prayer, read His Word, and trust that He is with you every step of the way. He is the ultimate healer, and He loves you more than you can imagine. In Isaiah 41:10, God says, "Do not fear, for I am with you; do not be dismayed, for I am your God. I will strengthen you and help you; I will uphold you with my righteous right hand." This promise is for you—no matter what you're going through, God is with you, and He will never let you go.

Final Thoughts: Hope and Healing After Trauma

As we close this chapter and this book, I want to leave you with a message of hope. Healing is possible. Peace is possible. Joy is possible. No matter how deep your pain, no matter how long you've been struggling, there is hope for a better future. I'm living proof of that.

The journey to healing is not easy, and there will be times when it feels like too much to bear. But I want you to remember that you are stronger than you think, and you are never alone. God is with you, and there are people who care about you and want to support you. Reach out to them, lean on them, and allow them to walk with you on this journey.

In closing, I want to share one of my favorite verses from the Bible, a verse that has given me so much hope and comfort over the years. It's from Romans 8:28, and it says, "And we know that in all things God works for the good of those who love him, who have been called according to his purpose." This verse reminds me that no matter what happens, God is at work in my life, bringing good out of even the most difficult circumstances. And I believe that He is doing the same in your life.

So, as you move forward from here, hold on to hope. Hold on to faith. And know that healing is not just possible—it's already happening. You are on a journey towards wholeness, towards peace, and towards a life filled with joy and purpose. Keep going, keep trusting, and keep believing that better days are ahead.

Thank you for allowing me to share my story with you, and for taking the time to walk this journey with me. I pray that this book has been a source of comfort, encouragement, and inspiration for you. May God bless you and keep you as you continue on your path to healing.

Appendices: Tools for Your Healing Journey

I want to leave you with some additional resources and tools to support you on your journey towards healing. The path to recovery is deeply personal, and it's important to have a variety of resources to draw upon as you continue to grow and heal. In this appendix, I've included some of the resources that have helped me, as well as exercises, journaling prompts, and inspirational quotes and affirmations that I hope will bring you comfort and encouragement.

Resources for Healing

When I was in the depths of my grief, I found solace in many different resources—books, websites, and support groups. These resources not only provided me with practical advice but also reminded me that I wasn't alone. Here are some of the ones that made a significant impact on my healing journey:

Books

> **"The Bible"**: This might seem obvious, but I can't overstate how much comfort and guidance I've found in Scripture. The Psalms, in particular, have been a source of immense strength for me.

Verses like Psalm 34:18, "The Lord is close to the brokenhearted and saves those who are crushed in spirit," remind me that God is always near, especially in times of pain.

"The Purpose Driven Life" by Rick Warren: This book helped me understand that there is a greater purpose behind everything we go through, even our pain. It's a wonderful resource for anyone seeking to understand their purpose in life.

"The Wounded Healer" by Henri Nouwen: This book explores the idea that our greatest wounds can also be a source of healing for others. Nouwen's reflections on suffering and healing resonated deeply with me and helped me see my own pain in a new light.

Websites

GriefShare: This is a Christian-based grief support group that offers in-person and online sessions. It's a great resource if you're looking for a community of people who understand what you're going through.

Focus on the Family: This website offers a wealth of resources on various topics, including grief, trauma, and emotional healing, all from a Christian perspective.

<u>Bible Gateway</u>: Whenever I needed a specific Bible verse to uplift my spirit, Bible Gateway was my go-to. It's an online Bible that allows you to search for verses by keyword, topic, or emotion.

Support Groups

Local Church Groups: Many churches offer support groups for those who are grieving or dealing with trauma. These groups can provide not only spiritual support but also a sense of community and belonging.

Celebrate Recovery: This Christian-based recovery program is designed for anyone struggling with hurts, hang-ups, and habits. It's a safe place to find healing and support within a community of believers.

Online Forums: There are many online forums where you can connect with others who are going through similar experiences. Websites like Reddit have dedicated communities for grief and trauma recovery where you can share your story and receive support.

Exercises and Journaling Prompts

Writing has always been a therapeutic outlet for me. It's a way to process emotions, gain clarity, and connect with God. Below are some exercises and journaling prompts that I've used to help me on my healing journey. I hope they can do the same for you.

Daily Gratitude Journal

Every morning or evening, write down three things you're grateful for. They don't have to be big things—sometimes the smallest blessings are the most meaningful. This practice can help shift your focus from pain to gratitude, reminding you of God's goodness in your life.

Example:

Today, I'm grateful for the comforting words of a friend.

I'm grateful for the warmth of the sun on my face.

I'm grateful for God's promise in Romans 8:28 that He works all things together for my good.

Letter to God

Write a letter to God about what you're going through. Pour out your heart to Him—your fears, your doubts, your pain. Then, spend some time listening for His response. You might find that writing this letter brings a sense of peace and clarity.

Prompt:

Dear God, today I'm feeling overwhelmed by the weight of my grief. I don't understand why this happened, and I'm struggling to find hope. Please give me the strength to get through this day and the peace to trust in Your plan for my life.

Scripture Reflection

Choose a verse that speaks to you and meditate on it throughout the day. Write about how this verse relates to your current situation and what God might be saying to you through it.

Prompt:

"For I know the plans I have for you," declares the Lord, "plans to prosper you and not to harm you, plans to give you hope and a future." (Jeremiah 29:11)

Reflect: How does this verse change the way I view my current struggles? What might God be trying to teach me through this difficult time?

Visualization Exercise

Close your eyes and imagine yourself in a peaceful place. It could be a beach, a forest, or a garden. Imagine Jesus is there with you, sitting beside you. What does He say to you? How does His presence make you feel? Write down your experience.

Prompt:

In my visualization, I saw Jesus sitting beside me on a quiet beach. He told me that I am not alone and that He is with me every step of the way. His presence brought a deep sense of peace and reassurance.

Healing Through Art

Sometimes words aren't enough to express what you're feeling. Try drawing, painting, or creating a collage that represents your journey. You don't have to be an artist—just let your emotions guide you.

Prompt:

Create a piece of art that represents your journey from darkness to light. What colors, shapes, or images come to mind? How does this creative process help you process your emotions?

Inspirational Quotes and Affirmations

I've always found that words have the power to uplift and inspire, especially during difficult times. Below are some of my favorite quotes and affirmations that have helped me stay grounded and hopeful.

Bible Verses

Isaiah 41:10: "So do not fear, for I am with you; do not be dismayed, for I am your God. I will strengthen you and help you; I will uphold you with my righteous right hand."

Psalm 46:1: "God is our refuge and strength, an ever-present help in trouble."

Romans 8:18: "I consider that our present sufferings are not worth comparing with the glory that will be revealed in us."

2 Corinthians 4:16-18: "Therefore we do not lose heart. Though outwardly we are wasting away, yet inwardly we are being renewed day by day. For our light and momentary troubles are achieving for us an eternal glory that far outweighs them all. So we fix our eyes not on what is seen, but on what is unseen, since what is seen is temporary, but what is unseen is eternal."

Quotes

"The wound is the place where the Light enters you." – Rumi: This quote reminds me that our deepest wounds are often the places where God's grace shines through most brightly.

"God never wastes a hurt." – Rick Warren: This is a powerful reminder that even our pain has a purpose in God's greater plan.

"Out of suffering have emerged the strongest souls; the most massive characters are seared with scars." – Kahlil Gibran: Our scars tell a story of survival, strength, and resilience.

Affirmations

I am a child of God, and He is with me through every trial.

I am stronger than I think, and I will overcome this.

God has a purpose for my pain, and He is working all things for my good.

I am healing, and every day brings me closer to peace and wholeness.

I trust in God's plan for my life, even when I don't understand it.

Final Thoughts

I want to remind you that healing is not a race—it's a journey that unfolds in its own time. Be patient with yourself, and remember that it's okay to have setbacks. What's important is that you keep moving forward, keep seeking out the support you need, and keep turning to God for strength and guidance.

You are not alone in this journey. God is with you, every step of the way. He sees your pain, He knows your struggles, and He is holding you in His loving arms. As you continue to heal, lean into His love and trust that He is working in your life, even when it feels like you're stuck in darkness.

Your journey towards healing is a testament to your strength and resilience. Every small step you take towards recovery is a victory, and every moment of doubt or difficulty is an opportunity for growth. Embrace your progress, no matter how small it may seem, and celebrate the victories along the way.

Remember the words of Romans 8:28: "And we know that in all things God works for the good of those who love him, who have been called according to his purpose." Even when it feels like your life is in disarray, trust that God is working behind the scenes to bring about a greater good. Your pain is not in vain; it's part of a greater story that God is writing for you.

Healing is not just about overcoming pain but also about discovering new aspects of yourself and growing closer to God. It's about finding hope in the midst of despair and allowing yourself to be transformed by the process. As you heal, let your experience be a source of inspiration and hope to others. Share your story, offer a listening ear, and be a beacon of light for those who are walking a similar path.

In closing, I want to leave you with a final thought from the book of Jeremiah 29:11: "For I know the plans I have for you," declares the Lord, "plans to prosper you and not to harm you, plans to give you hope and a future." These words remind us that God's plans for us are filled with hope and promise, even when our current circumstances seem bleak.

May you continue to find peace, joy, and purpose as you navigate your healing journey. Embrace each day with hope, knowing that God's love and grace are ever-present. Your story is still unfolding, and there is a beautiful future ahead, filled with healing and new beginnings. You are stronger than you know, and God is with you every step of the way.

Thank you for allowing me to share my journey with you. I pray that it has brought you comfort and hope. May you find the strength to continue forward and the courage to embrace the healing that lies ahead. God bless you on your journey.